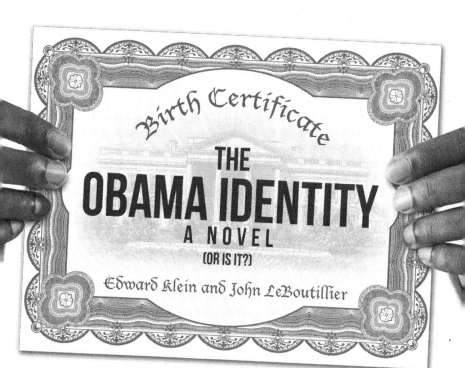

Birth Certificate

THE OBAMA IDENTITY

A NOVEL

(OR IS IT?)

Edward Klein and John LeBoutillier

ISBN: 1453792899
EAN-13: 9781453792896
LCCN: 2010913137

"Obama is George W. Bush's fault."

—Anonymous

PROLOGUE

"The-o-*dore*, hightail it over here and don't fanny around!"

There was no mistaking the husky faux-British accent on the other end of the phone line. It belonged to Whitney Nutwing, my boss at the CIA.

"What's up?" I asked.

"Command performance!" he replied. "*Very* urgent."

I slid into my 1964 Bentley Continental "Chinese Eye" Fixed Head Coupe with the luxe mahogany cockpit and drove over to Nutwing's office. He operated out of a safe house on Tracy Place in the fancy Sheridan-Kalorama section of Washington, D.C. The place was practically a CIA Historic Landmark. Each June, Nutwing threw a cocktail party in his corner office overlooking Dupont Circle. A select group of agents was treated to drinks, canapés, and a bird's-eye view of the Capitol's annual LGBT (Lesbian, Gay, Bisexual, and Transgender) Pride Parade. While we watched the parade, Nutwing played his favorite CD—Dropkick Murphy's *Citizen CIA*.

When I arrived at Whitney Nutwing's office, he was waiting for me at the door with an outstretched arm and a moist handshake.

"Good to see you…good to see you," he said, repeating himself, as was his habit. "Come right in…come right in. Join me by the window, The-o-*dore*. You'll be more comfortable there… *much* more comfortable."

Nobody *ever* called me Theodore except my mother, and then only on the rare occasion when she was completely sober. Whitney Nutwing's drawn-out pronunciation of my Christian name was getting under my skin. Which, knowing Nutwing, was exactly what he intended.

He was a living legend in the CIA. He had made his bones in Rome, where he had garroted his KGB counterpart with a piano wire and dumped the body into the Tiber with a note that said: *Sic semper tyrannosaurus*. His admirers conveniently overlooked the mangling of the Latin phrase *Sic semper tyrannis*. He was also famous for staving off a Communist takeover of Italy, thus clearing the way for the sixty-two incompetent and corrupt pro-American governments that have ruled Italy since World War II.

As Nutwing led me across his office, I noticed the meat hooks hanging from the ceiling. They were part of his collection of memorabilia from the execution of Benito Mussolini. Those two meat hooks had been used to hang the bodies of Il Duce and his mistress, Clara Petacci, upside down at a gas station just outside Lake Como in 1945. Word around the office was that

Nutwing identified with Il Duce, and that he kept the meat hooks on prominent display as a reminder of the fate that lay in store for those who ran afoul of his intimidating Il Duce-like outbursts of temper.

And he *was* an intimidating figure—a blimp of a man who weighed more than three hundred and fifty pounds. Like a lot of overweight people, Nutwing could exude good humor, bonhomie, and a kind of deceptive innocence. He reminded me of the cartoon character Baby Huey, the diapered, oversized duckling in *Quack a Doodle Doo*, who would exclaim, "I think you're trying to kill me" just before he finished you off.

He wore a baggy off-the-rack suit that didn't quite make it around his enormous midsection. As a devoted follower of men's fashion, I knew Nutwing would look much smarter in a made-to-measure Brioni. But I wasn't about to tell him that. One of the first things I was taught when I joined the CIA was *not* to give away precious information.

Once Nutwing seated me on his plush sofa, right under the meat hooks, he looked at me for a long time before speaking.

"How *are* you...The-o-*dore*?" he asked, every drawn-out syllable dripping with false sincerity.

"I'm fine," I said. "But call me Higgy."

"Oh, yes, how absentminded of me... how absent... *minded*," he said. "Higgy it is, of course! Theodore J. Higginbothem III. A fine name! A glorious family lineage! Well... Higgy... Do you know what next Monday is?"

"The beginning of the work week?" I guessed.

"It's Labor Day, 2008," he said. "The presidential election campaign is about to shift into high gear. I sent for you because I want you to go to Phoenix for a meeting with John McCain, who's trailing Barack Obama badly in the polls. Nothing less than the fate of our Republic hangs on the outcome of this presidential election. I trust you will accept the assignment… I trust…"

"I accept," I said, glancing up nervously at the meat hooks.

"Well then, Godspeed, The-o-dore….um, I mean Higgy. Godspeed! And remember what that great American rocketeer, Wernher von Braun, said: '*Scheitern ist keine Option!*' "

I nodded glumly. I speak several foreign languages, including Wernher von Braun's native tongue, Waffen-SS. With the English translation of his immortal words ringing in my ears—"*Failure is not an option!*"—I set off on my new mission.

When I returned to my house—my empty house, now that my wife Taitsie had absconded—I packed my enormous suitcase. Notwithstanding the blistering heat in Phoenix, I never traveled without at least three suits, with six matching ties to suit my mood. By the time I closed the suitcase, I could barely lift the monster. I cracked a private smile. The airline might charge for my luggage, but I was going to get my money's worth.

My mood sobered, however, during the long flight. By the time I arrived in Phoenix, I was feeling pressure in the base of my neck and the pit of my stomach. I get like that when I accumulate a lot of stress, which builds up toxins and weakens my immune system. And so, in preparation for my heart-to-heart with the Republican nominee, I booked a 90-minute lymphatic massage and colonic irrigation in the Alvadora Spa at the Royal Palms Resort, a five-star hotel in Phoenix.

After the spa treatment, I slipped on a fresh yellow-and-blue striped shirt with a white spread color and cuffs, a tartan plaid necktie, and a tan-and-brown Italian linen houndstooth sports jacket. Thus attired, I felt confident I was better dressed than anybody in the Greater Phoenix Metropolitan Area, especially those illegal immigrants who put the money they saved by dodging taxes into their wardrobes. I took the elevator down to the Royal Palms' lobby to wait for the McCain campaign escort who was scheduled to pick me up.

I was expecting the usual nearsighted poly-sci major in torn jeans, flip-flops, and unwashed hair. But the woman who approached me certainly didn't fit that description. She was a cotton-candy-hair blonde, and she was dressed in a Spandex cheerleader's uniform—short shorts, a skimpy, navel-baring halter-top, and knee-high white leather boots. I couldn't help thinking what good taste Senator McCain had.

"Hi, I'm Skylar," she said, "and I'm here to take you to see The Boss."

"H-hi," I stammered, flustered by her bodacious appearance.

"That's Skylar with an *a* not an *e*," she informed me.

I never quibble about spelling when my mouth goes dry, and I let her lead me outside to a black Chevrolet Suburban. Leaning up against a fender was her friend, a tall brunette by the name of Tara.

"Hello, Handsome," Tara said.

"Doesn't he look just like George Clooney?" Skylar asked.

"Better," said Tara. "He's not so swarthy."

I had never thought about it that way, but she was absolutely right. I got in the back, and the three of us set off for the trip to Sedona. With my usual sleuthing skills, I gathered from their endless prattle that Skylar was my sole escort. She had asked her friend to tag along to recruit Tara for the Arizona Sparrows cheerleading squad. During my career at the CIA (which I like to think of as the cheerleading squad for the U.S. of A.), I've done my share of recruiting. So I had a professional interest in listening to Skylar make her pitch.

"I'm so blessed to be on the cheerleader squad," Skylar said. "It's given me, like, so many amazing opportunities in life."

"*Opportunities*?" Tara asked. "Like what?"

"Like going to the jungles of Guatemala to shoot the 2008 Sparrows Cheerleaders Calendar."

"Omygod!" Tara said. "That's totally radical."

The jungles of Guatemala were also a big seller with CIA recruits. But the CIA didn't put out an annual calendar. Maybe we were missing out on something. I'd have to talk to Nutwing about that. I wouldn't mind seeing Valerie Plame on a "Girls of the CIA" wall calendar.

"And," Skylar added, "like being given the fabulous opportunity of being the month of August."

"You're *THIS* month?" Tara said.

"Yes," Skylar said, "this *MONTH*!"

And she started squealing.

And then Tara started squealing.

And then both of them were squealing at the top of their lungs, and jiggling in their seats, and waving their fingers in some kind of secret Arizona Sparrows' hand signal, and letting out earsplitting yelps.

"*Go Big Purple! Go Big Purple!*"

I tried to tune out their conversation, but that proved harder than expected, since every few minutes, Skylar shouted out another "*Go Big Purple!*" and pounded the car horn, jumped up and down in the driver's seat, and jerked the steering wheel violently. From my perch in the backseat, I could only hope the rapture would subside soon.

After a while, Skylar reached into the glove compartment, and produced a bottle of crème de menthe. As she and Tara took turns drinking from the bottle, I had a sudden feeling of *déjà vu*. Where had I met these two before? Then I realized that they reminded me of Susan Sarandon and Geena Davis in *Thelma & Louise*. The resemblance was accentuated when Tara (the Thelma character) stuck her bare feet out of the passenger-side open window and shouted: "No matter what happens, I'm glad I came with you!"

"Me, too," I said, lying. I felt certain the car would soon be hurtling over a roadside cliff.

It was obvious that Skylar and Tara had not a clue about the purpose of my visit with The Boss, as they called John McCain. My meeting was so hush-hush that no mention of it had been put on McCain's daily schedule, which was handed out by his press secretary to the dozen or so print and TV jackals that stalked him wherever he went. It was my guess that McCain used girls like Skylar to throw the media off the scent when he had a secret visitor like me.

For the next couple of hours, I settled back and eavesdropped on Skylar ("growing up, I took, like lots and lots of classes in cheerleading"). I idly watched the red rock slopes and the sweeping valleys of Scenic Route 89A whiz by—sometimes on two wheels—at 75 miles per hour.

As we neared Sedona, Tara twisted around in the shotgun seat and faced me.

"Are you actually going to *meet* The Boss?" she asked, sounding incredulous.

"Yes, I am," I replied.

"Skylar's a campaign volunteer in the McCain campaign," Tara said. "Can you imagine that?"

"No, I can't," I said, this time telling the truth.

"But she's never actually *met* The Boss," Tara added.

"That's right," Skylar said, flashing me a sad smile in the rearview mirror. "Like you're blessed to be able to meet The Boss. He's so Chuck Norris."

We soon pulled up at our destination a few miles west of Sedona on the banks of Oak Creek. The sun was high in the western sky, and its rays reflected off the brass-colored navy flight wings stenciled on the mailbox, which marked the entrance to McCain's ranch. The place was crawling with Secret

Service whispering into their sleeves and wearing their customary Ray-Bans.

We headed down a dusty dirt road past the parking area, where I noticed a black Escalade with its tailgate down, and two Secret Service chase cars. The Escalade displayed a flag with eight gold stars, forming the Big Dipper and the North Star, on a dark blue field. My son Vier's seventh-grade class had recently studied the flags of the fifty states, and I recognized the pennant on the Escalade's bumper as the state flag of Alaska.

That struck me as strange. What was even stranger, however, was the presence of several giggling teenagers—one of them obviously pregnant—and their mother, an attractive woman in her mid-forties who, despite the wall-to-wall security, was sitting on the edge of the tailgate, her pencil skirt hiked up to mid-thigh, cleaning a Remington shotgun.

As my car slowed down to make a turn, Tara pulled in her feet and pointed out the open window at the woman with the shotgun. "I'd like to do my hair just like hers."

"That's a snap," Skylar said. "You just gotta back comb your hair, then smooth it, make a half ponytail, clip it up, and arrange the hair so the clip doesn't show."

"Since when are you Harriet Hair-Do?" asked Tara.

"When you're one of the cheerleader captains, you've got to know lots of stuff," Skylar replied with undisguised pride. "Hey, "she added, nodding toward the woman with the up-do hairstyle, "check out her peep-toe shoes. How cool is that?"

The question was still echoing in my ears as we approached what Skylar described as The Boss's guest bungalow—a sprawling adobe house that was more elaborate than any bungalow I'd ever seen. Two more Secret Service agents stood guard and when I got out of the car they wanded me and took away my BlackBerry. I guessed The Boss didn't like people checking their messages while he was talking.

Skylar hopped out of the car, adjusted her halter-top so only the top half of her breasts were showing, and led me to the front door.

"Wait inside, Handsome," she said. "The Boss'll be over to see you in a jiff."

She reached up and gave me a peck on the cheek, and slipped me her Arizona Sparrows Cheerleaders business card.

"Give me a call sometime," she said with a wink. "My cell phone number's on the back of the card."

As I watched Skylar shimmying down the front path in her Spandex short shorts and knee-high white boots, I knew that I would *not* be calling her. Maybe other men would crave a roll in the hay with a statuesque and willing blonde like Skylar, but I had higher standards. I would only allow myself to stare ravenously until she disappeared from sight.

I walked inside the guest bungalow, making note of the Native American rugs on the floor, the potted cactuses, the walls covered with photographs of famous people—presidents, world leaders, and Arizonan sports stars like Randy Johnson, Curt Schilling and the boxer Mike Tyson. (I recalled that

McCain loved boxing and wanted the Feds to regulate it.) With mild horror I perused some photographs of McCain's wife dressed in bright neon-colored leather outfits.

My tour was interrupted when I heard the front door open and close. Two Secret Service agents came into the living room, both in casual attire. They did a quick visual sweep and disappeared. I merited no more interest than one of the potted saguaro cactus. A moment later, in walked McCain himself. He was a lot shorter than I remembered from the few times I had stood in the back of Senate Intelligence Committee briefings, while he sat up on a raised dais. Close up, you could see the throbbing muscle in his jaw. His fists clenched and unclenched. He looked like he wanted to smack somebody in the face.

I had expected a nice handshake and a little casual chit-chat. After all, he had been running for elective office for the past twenty-six years. You'd think he had the personal small-talk stuff down pat. But apparently not. All he said to me—without even making eye contact—was: "Let me see what ya got."

He sat down across from me in a worn leather chair. I opened my briefcase and removed a three-inch-thick black notebook—the focus of my work for the past four years. The cover was stenciled with a title—The Obama Identity—and the contents were tabbed and divided chronologically, from birth to the present.

With his short, bent arms, McCain grabbed the notebook out of my hands and plopped it down in his lap. He started to read the file. I noticed he twitched a lot. His beady little eyes darted all over the place. He read without emotion. No head nodding, no head shaking, no nothing.... After a while, he stopped reading and started skimming the file, rapidly turning the pages without possibly being able to absorb its contents.

What a shame, I thought. The file contained four years' worth of work by a team of crack CIA agents whom I had dispatched all over the world. Resting there on McCain's lap was political dynamite—the truth about Barack Obama's birth; the secret of his Muslim faith; the real story behind his relationship with "God-damn America" Reverend Jeremiah Wright and "let's blow up the Pentagon" William Ayres; and Obama's plan to weaken our country's military-industrial complex.

Any of the material, if made public, would automatically sink Obama and guarantee that this little man with the short arms and beady eyes sitting across the room from me in Sedona, Arizona, would become the forty-fourth President of the United States. I couldn't be prouder of my stealthy undercover talents. But after just ten minutes, McCain slammed the cover shut, stood up, and handed the file back to me.

"I don't ever want to see this again," he snarled. "Or hear about it, or what's in it. This meeting never happened. My staff will take you back to Phoenix. Good-bye, Mr. Higginbothem."

And with that, McCain was gone.

After I caught my breath, I looked out the window and watched McCain double-timing down the front path of his bungalow. Waiting for him at the curb was the woman I had seen earlier walking around with an upswept hair-do and a Remington shotgun—Alaska's Governor Sarah Palin. She was introducing McCain to her pregnant daughter, Bristol, and a young man with a redneck mullet hairstyle—short at the front and sides and long in the back.

I couldn't hear what McCain was saying, but I saw him motion to Palin to follow him to a small U-Haul truck parked a few yards away. A McCain aide opened the back door of the truck, lowered a ramp, and wheeled out two large garment racks with a wardrobe of expensive women's clothing. Palin examined the clothes, jumped up and down with delight, threw her arms around McCain, and gave him a big hug.

I didn't feel so charitably minded. All my good work, dismissed with a flick of his hand. The lot of a spy was truly a thankless one.

As I headed back to Phoenix, I stared out the window at Scenic Route 89A, and went over in my mind the meeting with McCain. Okay, I thought, he doesn't want to use the information I've collected about Obama. Okay, I thought, he doesn't want the American people to know what the real Obama is like. Well, there was nothing surprising about that. After all, McCain always had an odd sense of honor about attacking Democrats. He had no qualms whatsoever about savaging his fellow Republicans, but for some reason he refused to lower the boom on Democrats....

Then it hit me.

Why worry about John McCain? *I had a higher calling.* It was my duty as a career intelligence officer to tell the American people all I had learned about Barack Obama. Whether they knew it or not, their taxes had paid for this investigation, and they might very well have to pay in a *different* kind of way for electing Obama as their next president. I owed it to the American people to reveal The Obama Identity.

BOOK ONE

CHAPTER ONE

I was born with a silver pistol in my mouth.

As a baby, I spent countless hours sucking the barrel of that Beretta, until I wore off its silver plate and started chipping my milk teeth on its hard edges and my nanny took the gun away. Some amateur psychiatrists might regard this pistol as my secret "Rosebud." Strangely, my oral fixation with the Beretta didn't leave me with a taste for Italian firearms. As an adult, I prefer the semi-automatic German Glock, even though it doesn't have the *fruity* flavor of the Beretta.

The pistol of my contented childhood belonged to my father, the mastermind of the CIA coup that returned the Shah of Iran to the Peacock Throne and toppled Iran's democratically elected government. Actually, my father's real claim to fame in the CIA came *after* he engineered the 1953 Iranian coup. He was something of a clotheshorse (a trait I inherited), and he imported a group of Bulgarian tailors to design a new uniform for the Shah to wear on state occasions. They came up with a design for a long white double-breasted worsted jacket with oversized gold-encrusted epaulets. I thought the uniform made the Shah look like a character in the Marx Brother's movie *Duck Soup*.

But the Shah loved his new uniform. He pinned a large gold nameplate to its right breast—it read SHAHANSHAH (KING OF KINGS)—and he found an excuse to wear it on every possible occasion. He even asked the Bulgarians to make a wet-suit version of the uniform, replete with waterproof gold-encrusted epaulets, so he could wear it while waterskiing in Biarritz with his second wife, Soraya Esfandiary-Bakhtiari, who was known, according to *her* nameplate, as the SHAHANBABU.

As proud as my father was of his achievements on the sartorial front, he was even prouder of his creation of SAVAK, the Shah's dreaded domestic intelligence service. He recruited all of the original members of SAVAK and trained them to torture the Shah's opponents by pulling out their nails, shoving electric cattle prods up their rectums, and dripping acid into their nostrils. I learned how to do Pilates on the wooden torture rack in the basement of the Sa'adabaad Palace. And it was there, in that dank basement, that one of the torturers taught me the hand-to-hand combat techniques of *Krav Maga*, the lethal Israeli martial art, with which you can disarm an opponent with a single swift blow.

All of this naturally made my father, Theodore J. Higginbothem II, a hero in the CIA. He was known affectionately as The Deuce, which was a kind of CIA code, because "The Deuce" could mean either "the second," or "the devil," as in "what the *deuce* are you trying to do?" Devil or not, I was proud to be named Theodore J. Higginbothem III, even if people ignored the three sticks after my name. They call me Higgy.

My father was away a lot, polishing his CIA cover as a successful trader in Middle East crude-oil futures. And although I lived under the same roof as my mother in the Chehel Sotoun Palace in Isfahan, the ancient capital of Iran, I rarely saw her. She preferred to stay in bed all day, guzzling gin, which was illegal in Muslim Iran, but which my father stored in huge quantities to keep her out of his hair. At times I would listen at the bedroom door. She rhapsodized so often about Gordon that for years I thought I had a missing brother.

During the first dozen or so years of my life I was brought up and cared for by a staff of bowing, scraping, sniveling servants in Chehel Sotoun Palace. I guess that's where I developed my lifelong desire to be treated in a princely fashion.

The palace was known as "The Pavilion of Forty Columns," because the twenty slender wooden columns supporting its entrance were reflected in the water of a large lily pond, which appeared to double their number. I learned to add, subtract, and multiply at the knee of my tutor, Pourushaspa Spitama, a bent and twisted old man with a bad lisp and a pair of bug eyes that looked off in opposite directions.

Spitama (whom I secretly nicknamed "Spit-on-Me") taught me to speak Farsi, the language of Iran. As part of his teachings, he introduced me to the esoteric philosophy of Iran's most famous ancient prophet and philosopher, Zarathustra, a name I could never pronounce properly.

"Dear little Higgy," Spit-on-Me would lisp, spraying spittle on my black velvet suit and white collar, "please pay attention! Zarathustra teaches us that the purpose of humankind is to apply constructive thoughts, words, and deeds to life. If we see something that appears to be unfortunate or evil, it's only because of our lack of *constructive thoughts*."

Old Spit-on-Me had a beautiful young wife by the name of Maidhyoimangha and by the time I was thirteen years old, I began to have *constructive thoughts* about her. Naturally, I did not give free rein to these prohibited thoughts. But Maidhyoimangha seemed able to read my mind, for one day she took me by the hand and led me to the reflecting pond of Chehel Sotoun Palace, and there she stripped off her *shalwar kameeze*, a long tunic and pants, and threw me into the pond and jumped in after me. This odd cleansing ritual happened on several occasions, and things were getting pretty constructive when one day Spit-on-Me suddenly appeared and found us rutting under the water lilies.

"What do you have to say for yourself, Higgy?" my father demanded to know when he confronted me with my offense.

"Dad, Spit-on-Me—I mean, Mr. Spitama—says that Sara Truth teaches us that when something appears to be wrong, it's only because of our lack of constructive thoughts."

"Higgy," my father said, "Spit-on-Me has been selling you a bill of Zarathustrian goods."

"Wow, you really know how to pronounce that guy's name," I said, impressed.

"Shut up!" he said. "Higgy, I know what your natural bent is. You want to dominate. It's natural, son. The world is full of people struggling against each other for one thing—*power.* That's how democracy got started. Democracy gives the poor, weak, sick and pathetic mob the *illusion* that they have power and that they're running things. Whereas in fact the mob has to be ruled by wealthy, strong, healthy and powerful men. Men like me! Men who make up the CIA!"

"But Dad..."

"Don't interrupt!" he raved. "Do you know what we call the CIA among ourselves when we're kicking back with a few brews? We call it Control-Influence-Authority."

"But Dad...."

Yet he was only warming up. "Higgy, consider yourself like Adam after the Fall. Like Yahweh, I'm expelling you from this Garden of Eden-like place and I'm sending you where they'll teach you how to rule the mob. How to exert control, influence, and authority. Pack your bags, Higgy. I'm shipping you off to the only prep school worth a lick of salt. You're going to Groton!"

CHAPTER TWO

I was always big for my age, and no sooner had I arrived on Groton's four-hundred-acre campus in Massachusetts than I was selected from a group of new boys to participate in the school's annual boxing tournament. On the chosen day, I climbed into the boxing ring and found myself staring across sixteen feet of blue canvas at my opponent, a glowering six-foot-five Goliath by the name of Brooks Biddle Peabody VIII. Brooks was the senior prefect, as the school's head boy was called, and he ruled the mob of three hundred Grotonians with the kind of authority that would have made my father proud.

Before the bell for the first round sounded, my roommate, Fatty Dickens, who was serving as my corner man, smeared some Vaseline over my eyebrows and whispered into my ear.

"Higgy," he said, "use your jab and stay as far away from this guy as possible. He's dangerous."

"What do you mean?" I asked.

"In last year's boxing tournament, Brooks picked a kid to fight him and the kid refused. Said he had a bad knee. But the truth was he was scared shitless to get into the ring with Brooks. So the night before the fight, Brooks went to the kid's room, dragged him out of bed, and said, 'Your *knee* hurts? Which knee?' When the kid hesitated, Brooks said, 'I'll make sure they *both* hurt!' And he stomped on both knees, sending the kid to Mass General."

Just then the bell rang. Brooks bolted out of his corner and swung a haymaker at my head. I ducked. But then Brooks, who was twice my size, shoved me into a neutral corner and began working my body with both fists like I was a big slab of cookie dough.

He didn't know I was trained by the best. Recalling my close-combat *Krav Maga*, I slipped to the side and slapped both of my gloves simultaneously against Brooks' ears.

In an instant, his arms dropped to his sides. Like a giant redwood, he slowly toppled forward and crashed face down on the canvas. In less than twenty seconds, I had won the fight.

I heard an upper classman mutter, "The little prick must be another CIA son."

The next day was Founder's Day, and at the closing ceremony, Brooks Biddle Peabody VIII pulled me aside.

"Listen, dipshit," he said, "you got in a lucky punch yesterday. But as a new boy, you still have to do what I order you."

"Sure, Brooks," I said. "No hard feelings."

"Not *much*," he said with a vengeful sneer. "Listen, I want you to put on your trench coat with nothing underneath. Not even your underwear. Just your birthday suit. Then I want you to go up to Mrs. Piddlehonor, the Headmaster's wife and when you have her full attention, say your name and introduce yourself—and flash her. Understand?"

"Whatever you say, Brooks," I said. "I'm a firm believer in doing the *constructive* thing."

An hour later, in front of the whole school, including the masters and their wives and dozens of distinguished alumni, I did as Brooks had instructed me. I walked up to Mrs. Piddlehonor and said, "Hi, I'm Theodore J. Higginbothem III and I am here to introduce myself." I whipped open my trench coat and exposed my considerable endowments.

A look of febrile interest entered her eyes, but a deafening silence fell over the Founder's Day crowd. Then I heard the angry voice of Mr. Piddlehonor, the Headmaster.

"Higginbothem," he bellowed, "you're expelled!"

CHAPTER THREE

Things were looking pretty grim for me until The Deuce came to the rescue. The CIA was packed to the gills with Old Grotonians, and The Deuce called in his chits with these big fish. He called his modus operandi "fish and chits."

The big fish phoned Mr. Piddlehonor, the indignant Headmaster, and told him to get over it.

"That's all fine and good," the Headmaster said, "but what about my *wife*?"

"It's unfortunate that she was submitted to such a public embarrassment," the Old Grotonian said.

"She wasn't *embarrassed*," the Headmaster said. "She was *confused*."

"Confused?"

"Yes," said Mr. Piddlehonor, "she was confused about how one of my young, lower-form students could be better endowed than I am!"

I was readmitted and allowed to stay at Groton for the next four years. During that time I paid no visits—no unsolicited visits, that is—to the Headmaster's house. And after graduation, I followed in The Deuce's footsteps once again and enrolled at Harvard University.

At the time, the Vietnam War was still Topic A on campus. There was revolution in the streets, kids were strung out on drugs, and many people thought America was coming apart at the seams. A few years before I arrived at Harvard, anti-war students occupied the main administration hall, and Nathan Pusey, the starched-shirt president of the university, called in the police. Many students were injured in the ensuing melee, and in response, the students called a protest strike that paralyzed the university. Shortly thereafter, Nathan Pusey announced his retirement.

With Pusey out of the way, members of the Harvard Board of Overseers, the university's senior governing board, instituted a new regime. They even gave it an official name. They called it the HARVARD ANTI-EVERYTHING MOVEMENT.

To start with, they abolished Parents Weekend, announcing "Parents are the root cause of fascist America." Then the Overseers replaced the annual Columbus Day celebration with "Native American Day," promulgating, "White men didn't discover this nation; they raped it." Then they canceled the football season, decreeing: "Violence begets violence." They filled the Harvard Stadium field with bushy marijuana plants and gave each student "pot stamps," which they could exchange for free marijuana cigarettes. And, of course, they expressly banned the CIA from recruiting on campus.

One day, The Deuce took me for drinks at his old club, The Porcellian, the most exclusive, blue-blooded club at Harvard. He was wearing his little golden pig pin, which symbolized "The Porc," as the club was nicknamed.

"You know, Higgy," he told me over gin martinis, "your grandfather, Theodore J. Higginbothem Sr., joined The Porc in 1915—the year before he joined the Lafayette Escadrille as a fighter pilot. He was shot down and killed on the German-French border with his Harvard pal and fellow Porcellian, Quentin Roosevelt, the youngest son of former President Teddy Roosevelt."

"Dad, you've told me this story a hundred times," I said.

"That's why I want you join this club," The Deuce said. "Every man at Harvard wants to get into Porcellian. If you want to become the kind of man I want you to be, you've got to be a Porc."

"What kind of man is that, Dad?"

"A *porc!* A *pig!*" he said. "A greedy, voracious, insatiable sonofabitch. A glutton for power. An acquisitive, covetous, avaricious bastard!" His shouting and wild gesticulations were drawing the eye of everyone in the place, and he caught himself. In a quieter voice he went on, "Remember what I told you when you were a kid in Iran? The world is full of evil people struggling against each other for one thing—*power*. The mob has to be ruled by wealthy, strong, healthy and powerful men. That's why I joined the Porcellian. And that's why I joined the CIA."

That was the first time The Deuce admitted to me that he worked for the CIA. Sitting in that musty old clubhouse on

Massachusetts Avenue, under the club's motto, *Dum vivimus vivamus* (WHILE WE LIVE, LET'S LIVE), he proceeded to tell me everything about his espionage work—past and present.

After our third martini, he said in a somewhat muzzy voice:

"I suppose you've figured out by now why I've been telling you all this."

"You want me to join the CIA," I said.

"Not exactly," he said. "I want you to do what we call 'light work' on the Harvard campus. Don't ask me any questions now. A man is going to call you. His name is Ralph. Follow his instructions."

CHAPTER FOUR

"Ralph" called a week later. He asked me to meet him the following night, at two o'clock in the morning, on the northern outskirts of the Fresh Pond Reservoir, in the parking lot of a nursing home called the Neville Center. He'd be driving a two-door Oldsmobile Cutlass, he informed me.

At the appointed hour, I arrived on my twelve-speed bike and found Ralph's Olds parked behind a dumpster in a remote corner of the nursing home lot. It was an overcast night with a light drizzle, pitch-black outside, and when I climbed into the car, I noticed that its overhead reading lamp didn't automatically go on. I couldn't make out Ralph's features, but I had the distinct impression that he was too old to be doing this kind of clandestine work.

"It's good to meet you, my boy," he said.

"Good to meet you, too, Ralph," I replied.

"Of course, that's not my actual Christian name," he said. "'Ralph' is what they call my *handle* in the CIA."

He had an old man's voice, too. Very cultured. Definitely upper class. The kind that rules the mob.

As I sat down in the front passenger seat, I landed on a hard, round object. I reached back and pulled it out. On it were printed phosphorescent letters that glowed in the dark: *Agent 15 – Diphosgene (DP) – 6 Oz.*

Ralph leaned over and snatched it away from me.

"I wish we had these tear gas grenades when those radical bastards seized control of the university president's office," he muttered. "A few of these nifty grenades, lobbed into that long-haired crowd, would have changed everything! We could have stopped them in their filthy tracks…."

He seemed agitated as he fiddled with the grenade. But then he let out a deep, mournful sigh and sunk into a long silence.

"Higgy," he said after he had recovered his composure, "what I'm going to ask you to do is very simple, but it's very important, and it's got to be done with the utmost discretion. Things have gotten out of hand here at Harvard. We have become the capital of radicalism and anti-Americanism. Every leftist comes here to recruit impressionable Harvard students. Russell Means, the radical Indian leader from South Dakota, wants students to pledge to give *all* their possessions – including their families' homes – to the Indians! The Black Panthers want automatic admission to Harvard for *all* ex-convicts. And the Weathermen are holding 'How to Make a Bomb in Your Dorm' seminars. Higgy, what I need you to do is show up like any other student at these meetings. Grab their literature, make some mental notes of who said what. Give me a flavor of what these leaders are saying and planning...."

He stopped to let this sink in.

"Okay?" he said, continuing to fiddle absent-mindedly with the tear-gas grenade.

"Sure," I said brightly. "Sounds *constructive*"

His voice took on a dolorous tone. "Higgy, do you have any idea how hard it's been?"

"How hard *what's* been?"

"Teaching here at Harvard," he said. "Do you have any idea what it's like to stand up in front of a lecture hall filled with women? Nubile young women wearing no bras or panties, their nipples at high beam? Women who are trying to distract you. Women who are... *giggling*! Can you imagine...*giggling at Harvard*? They intentionally try to make you lose your place in your lecture notes."

I didn't know what to say.

He continued: "Or when you're a dorm master and at three o'clock in the morning the smell of pot is so strong that it wakes you up and you look out and see students having an orgy in the courtyard and when you call the Harvard cops to break it up, the cops join in!"

He was growing more agitated by the second, and his voice was reaching higher and higher registers.

"Higgy, as much as I deplore these libertine ways.... I have to admit that *sometimes* I wished it was *me*—I mean, I wished it *were* me—or *I*—or whatever—I wished I was screwing all those girls and *me* getting higher than a kite. Ah, there I've said it! I've confessed! Yes, I wanted to get into those lamb pots!"

"Lamb pots?" I said.

Abruptly, "Ralph" put out his hand to shake mine and, in the darkness, dropped the tear gas grenade. I heard it hit the carpeted floor and roll around.

"Damn!" he exclaimed as he reached down in the darkness

I could hear his agitated breathing as he searched around the car floor.

"It's stuck behind the emergency brake. Here...I think I've got it."

I heard a small "click," which I knew was trouble. Ralph had inadvertently pulled the pin. In five seconds the car would be filled with an explosion of tear gas. I yanked open my door.

"Ralph," I shouted, "get out now!"

I flew out the door and dashed away from the car. Ralph was older – and slower. He barely had the car door open when a distinctive *thwump!* erupted and then a billowing cloud of white tear gas filled the car.

In his panicked escape he inadvertently pressed the car's horn. In an instant, lights came on in a wing of the nursing home, bathing the parking lot in a glow.

I finally got a good look at "Ralph."

He was Nathan Pusey, the former president of Harvard.

CHAPTER FIVE

After college, I read law at the University of Oxford for a couple of years, which provided me with a convenient cover to infiltrate anti-American protest groups. At the end of my time there I fell madly in love. I met Elizabeth Millard, the fabulous, breathtaking, amazing "Taitsie."

I've always thought our meeting was kismet. It was July 4, 1979, and I had just graduated from Oxford. Although I didn't realize it at the time, I was probably on the lookout for a wife to complete the picture in my mind of American manhood: job, home, wife, kids, and erectile dysfunction.

I can recall the exact moment I laid eyes on Taitsie. We were standing at the opposite ends of a large, crowded room full of tipsy American ex-pats, who had been invited to celebrate Independence Day at the United States Embassy in London. You could never miss Taitsie in a crowd. She was taller than all the other women, far more beautiful, and she always attracted a cluster of hyperventilating suitors.

Her charms were on full display that afternoon. She had the glossiest black hair I had ever seen; natural, unplucked eyebrows that went straight across her forehead; and a smile that promised…well, to be honest, I didn't know quite what her smile promised. If I had known, I might not have married her.

While Taitsie was flirting with her male admirers, she looked over in my direction, and our eyes met—not once, but two or three times. I was drinking like a fish in those days, but the booze never helped much when it came to having courage with beautiful women. And so when this raven-haired beauty marched over to me and looked me straight in the eye, I took another slug of my double Dewar's on the rocks and gazed back at her in a state of mute catatonia.

"Hello," she finally said when she realized that, unlike all the other men at the cocktail reception, I wasn't going to make a pass at her.

"H-h-hi," I managed to stammer. "I'm Theodore J. Higginbothem III."

"You've got to be kidding," she said.

"No, I'm serious."

"That can't *possibly* be your *real* name."

"I'm afraid it *is*," I said. "But my friends call me Higgy."

"Well, I hardly qualify as your friend."

"You will," I said, and was immediately shocked at my unaccustomed boldness.

"Are you sure?"

"I think so," I said, worried now that I had gone too far.

"When did you decide that we were going to be friends?"

"As soon as I caught your eye," I said. "I knew we were going to be *more* than friends."

Holy shit! I thought. This doesn't sound like me. I'd never spoken to a woman like this in my entire life. There was something about this woman that knocked me off the rails. I was bowled over by my audacity. So, apparently, was she.

"Well, Higgy...." she said.

She hesitated for a moment, as though she was searching for words. Then she did something extraordinary. She put her arm through my arm, waved good-bye to her admirers, and led me to a far corner of the room. Up close, I noticed that there was a little too much white in her eyes, which might have explained the hint of recklessness that I had detected in her smile.

"I've always thought that self-confidence was a man's most attractive quality," she said. "So, allow me to introduce myself. I'm Elizabeth Dubois Millard. *My* friends call me Taitsie. And, in case you're interested, my father is your host. He's standing over there under that American flag. That's him—Robert Millard, the ambassador to the Court of St. James's."

Now *I* was truly speechless.

The Deuce had told me all about "Ducky" Millard and his ongoing turf war with the CIA station chief in the London embassy. Ducky was a classic case of the egotistical businessman who was rewarded for his generous campaign contributions with a plum ambassadorship. But he had made the fatal mistake of attacking the Agency in his dispatches to

Washington. Ergo, Ducky became the target of a concerted CIA campaign designed to discredit and disgrace him. Among other things, CIA investigators found out that Ducky had condoned a sexual affair between his 25-year-old daughter Taitsie and his old Princeton roommate, Richard Hack, who was more than twenty years Taitsie's senior.

The next day, I put in a call to The Deuce over the secure CIA trans-Atlantic phone line. He was alarmed to hear that I had fallen head over heels for Ducky Millard's daughter Taitsie.

"Higgy, listen to me—you must n*ever* see this girl again," he said. "Her whole blasted family is persona non grata in the CIA."

"Sure, Dad," I said. "Thanks for the constructive advice."

However, for the first time in my life, I had absolutely no intention of listening to my father. Something had happened to me—something that liberated me from his paternal thrall. As soon as I hung up with The Deuce, I phoned Taitsie.

"I can't wait to see you again," I told her.

CHAPTER SIX

From then on, I was living a double lie. I kept my romance with Taitsie a secret from The Deuce, and I kept my undercover work for the CIA a secret from Taitsie.

In the summer of 1980, The Deuce called from D.C.

"Higgy," he said, "I need you here. *Now.* Can't talk about it on the phone."

I was on the next plane from Heathrow to Dulles, where The Deuce met me in a limo and took me to an office building in Rosslyn, just across the Potomac from D.C. Inside, there were signs all over the place that proclaimed: NATIONAL CAMPAIGN HQ FOR OUR NEXT PRESIDENT—RONALD REAGAN! 1980.

In a corner office on the top floor, The Deuce introduced me to Reagan's campaign manager, who turned out to be my father's old friend, William J. Casey. During World War II, The Deuce and Casey had roomed together in London, where they worked for the Office of Strategic Services (OSS), the precursor of the CIA.

I had heard from The Deuce that Casey was a nice fellow, but I found him hard to size up. He mumbled so badly that I couldn't be sure what he was saying. Clearly, he was born to be a spy, because he had a built-in scrambler in his mouth.

"Genelmun, pease be sheeted," Casey began. "Me and The Douche go back a long way," he said, mangling my father's nickname. "You're here cuz we're nine moss into the Rain hostage crisis, and fifty-three Mericun embiss pussonnel are still held by the Ranians. According to our poring"—and here, he pounded a four-inch thick stack of polling data—"the presidential lexsun hinges on one thin. If Prezdun Jimminy Carter gets the hostages out before Noveber, he wins. If not, we win. Pe-iud."

Casey hesitated, then added: "I'm sure that The Douche grees with me."

The Deuce nodded his assent, and then spoke up.

"Higgy, what Bill is trying to say is, would you be willing to make a secret little visit to Iran with me? You speak fluent Farsi, thanks to your old tutor, Spit-on-Me. I don't speak the lingo. I need someone I can completely trust to help me talk to Ayatollah Khomeini."

I was flabbergasted. First my father had crowned a king in Iran, and now he wanted to crown a king right here at home.

Fifty-three American hostages were being held at the mansion of Iran's notorious former secret police chief, Teymour Bakhtiari, where they were kept in solitary confinement, forbidden to speak to one another, and repeatedly threatened with execution. Bill Casey wanted us to go to Iran to *stop* the Iranian government from releasing these poor, tormented hostages.

After we left Casey's office, and were driving back to D.C., I expressed my misgivings to The Deuce.

"Higgy," he said, "just remember how Jimmy Carter screwed up the Desert One helicopter mission to rescue our hostages. The man's a total twit. He's not competent to be president. Four more years of that hick peanut farmer, and the country may never recover. If you and I pull this one off for Bill Casey and Ronald Reagan, we'll be doing the country a favor. It's our patriotic *duty* to stop the Iranians from releasing the American hostages."

Was *that* what was meant by constructive thinking?

CHAPTER SEVEN

I was happy to join The Deuce for the secret meeting with Grand Ayatollah Ruhollah Mousavi Khomeini, the Supreme Leader of the Islamic Republic of Iran. This was my first trip back to Iran since 1966, when I was thirteen years old and The Deuce had forced me to dump Old Spit-on-Me's bodacious young wife Maidhyoimangha and go off to school at Groton. It was a strange homecoming, full of conflicting emotions. This assignment—to keep the American hostages locked up in Iran—was making it hard for me to swallow the constructive philosophy of Iran's ancient prophet and philosopher, Sara Truth. I seemed to be communing more with the evil in the world.

We flew from Washington, D.C., to London, and then on to Istanbul, Damascus, and Tehran. There, we transferred to the Ayatollah's private jet, which whisked us off to Qum, known for its holiness, not its hot sex. We arrived in Qum on September 29 1980, just one week after Iraq's dictator, Saddam Hussein, had launched a full-scale invasion of Iran. The Iranians were on a war footing and were naturally suspicious of all foreigners, fearing that we might be agents working for Saddam. We were forced to submit to a body-cavity search by a fat, sweaty Iranian security guard who resembled Marlon Brando and had obviously seen Brando's notorious butter scene in *Last Tango in Paris.*

The Deuce and I were taken to a windowless room, where we encountered one of the Ayatollah's aides, a short, menacing-looking university student named Mahmoud Ahmadinejad. He was the ringleader of the so-called "students" who had seized our embassy and were holding the hostages.

"In order to prepare properly for your audience with the Grand Ayatollah," Ahmadinejad proclaimed, "you will first be required to make a spiritual pilgrimage to the sanctuary of Fatima al-Masumeh, the Infallible One."

"Will we have to take our shoes off?" The Deuce asked in alarm.

"Of course," Ahmadinejad snarled.

"I've got a hole in my sock," explained The Deuce, ever the fastidious fashion plate.

"Not to worry," Ahmadinejad said. "Performing such a pilgrimage guarantees that you will go to Paradise and make love with a dozen virgins, even if you have *two* holes in your socks."

He flashed a malicious smile, then added: "Of course, if you were a Jew, those holes might take on a completely different meaning."

"Paradise is fine," said The Deuce. "And a dozen virgins is even better. But we just don't want to end up as hostages numbers fifty-four and fifty-five."

Ahmadinejad shot The Deuce an indignant look.

"The Imam has given you his *word*," he said. "We only kidnap civilians, not CIA agents who once told us how to run our country."

CHAPTER EIGHT

We were taken to the private estate of Grand Ayatollah Ruhollah Mousavi Khomeini, the Supreme Leader. I was in for quite a shock. To the outside world, the Ayatollah was an ascetic living in a humble tent. In reality, he lived in indescribable luxury in a sprawling marble palace, waited on hand and foot by a legion of servants. In our honor, he laid out a sumptuous banquet that featured three cuisines—Iranian, French, and American—and an endless supply of Cristal Brut "Methuselah" champagne.

"Drink up!" Ayatollah Khomeini commanded. "I bought this champagne at a Sotheby's auction for $17,625 a bottle."

The place setting in front of the Ayatollah consisted of a spoon—the only utensil he ever used. The banquet was served by a dozen young waitresses dressed in loose black *burkas*, which covered their entire bodies but were slit up the sides to their waist. The waitresses were completely nude underneath, and most of them ended up with red rear ends from the frequent slaps they received on their buttocks when they bent over the low table to serve the guests. I was about to try it myself when I was stopped by a murderous glower from one of the holy men.

After the feast, we adjourned to a small prayer room, which was carpeted with priceless Persian rugs. The Great Man carried his champagne glass with him, and was accompanied by his handpicked president, Bani Sadr, and our menacing-looking student guide, Mahmoud Ahmadinejad. Khomeini didn't waste any time getting down to business.

"I am quite receptive to hearing what incentives you have in mind to induce us to keep the American hostages in Iran until after your presidential election," he said in Farsi, which I translated for The Deuce. "I want Jimmy Carter defeated as much as you do. I despise any man who commits adultery only in his heart."

As Ayatollah Khomeini continued with his monologue, I began to detect a strange smell, which soon became overpowering. I turned to Ahmadinejad and whispered to him in English:

"What's that awful smell?"

"It's the Ayatollah," he whispered in English. "Whenever he eats spicy foods, he gets chronic flatulence."

"Let me tell you," I said back, keeping my voice low. "I would do anything for my country, but sitting in a small, unventilated prayer room with a seventy-year old fart machine who's just eaten some under-cooked Persian lamb is almost too much to bear."

"Tell me about it," Ahmadinejad said. We were brothers in spirit at last. "The next time we need to put down an uprising by political dissidents, we won't have to use poison gas. We'll just send in the Imam."

Meanwhile, the Ayatollah was addressing the subject of incentives.

"As you know," he said, "we are at war with the Devil himself, Saddam Hussein. Tehran is being attacked by air every night. We could use your help."

The Deuce had been briefed by Bill Casey and was authorized to make a tempting offer.

"Eminence," he said, "assuming Ronald Reagan becomes the President of the United States, and assuming you promise to keep the American hostages in captivity until then, I'm authorized to tell you that certain military assets could be made available—medium-range missiles capable of reaching Baghdad, for example..."

Khomeini waited for the translation and nodded his assent. He then turned to me.

"Speaking of missiles," he said, "perhaps there is something more your father could do for me."

I translated for The Deuce.

"Of course, Eminence. How can we help?" The Deuce said.

Lowering his voice almost to a whisper, the Ayatollah said, "Last year while living in Paris, I read about some promising new drug that was in the experimental phase. I think it was called sildenafil citrate. It helps a man launch his *own* missile."

"Ah!" The Deuce said, immediately grasping the Ayatollah's meaning. "Higgy, tell the Imam that a Swiss company is conducting trials on erectile dysfunction as we speak. I think I can secure some of this product for the Ayatollah."

When I had completed the translation, the Spiritual Guide smiled. We had reached a common understanding. He raised his glass of champagne in a toast—"To lust beyond the heart!" he shouted—and then downed its contents with one deep contented swallow.

CHAPTER NINE

Ronald Reagan was elected president, Bill Casey was appointed director of Central Intelligence, and I was given a new boss to report to at the CIA—Whitney Nutwing.

Our first meeting got off to a bad start.

"My, my, you don't look at *all* like your father," said Nutwing. "But I can see the resemblance to your mother. How *is* that *poor* woman?"

I detected an insult buried somewhere in the remark. But I was too busy staring at the meat hooks hanging from the ceiling to pay much attention.

"My m-mother is...the *same*," I stammered.

That was in fact true. My mother was a fulltime resident at Silver Hill, an expensive dry-out in Connecticut for rich drunks.

"Your mother was quite a beauty in her day," Nutwing said, "if a little bit too *corybantic* for her own good. *Corybantic*—C-O-R-Y-B-A-N-T-I-C: look it up in the dictionary. But as her son, I suppose you don't want to hear about *that* side of your mother.... Come, join me by the window. If my research is correct, your brand of drink is Hidalgo Manzanilla Pastrana sherry."

I didn't think it wise to drink during this first meeting with my new boss, so I declined.

"*Un momento*," he said, holding up a warning finger.

Uh-oh, I thought. He's switching to Italian. Alarm bells went off in my head. I had been warned to be on guard whenever Nutwing started spouting Italian

"Higgy," he said, "lesson number one: a good agent *never* passes up an opportunity to drink. Why? Because it loosens the mouth of the person *offering* the drink."

He handed me a glass of sherry and then guided me over to his overstuffed green sofa. He collapsed into his seat and the cushion emitted a loud sigh.

He looked me over for quite some time, particularly in the groin area, and then said, "Higgy, you need a cover…"

I looked down at my slacks and checked to see if my fly was open.

"No, not *that*!" he said. "A cover…a *legend*…a profession that will hide the true nature of your agency work. Any ideas?"

"Not really," I replied.

Nutwing sipped his drink and then asked, "If you weren't a CIA agent, what would you most like to be?"

"A writer, I suppose."

He chuckled loudly.

"I've read your Harvard senior thesis on '*How Constructive Thinking Could Have Prevented the American Revolution*,' " he said. "Believe me, Higgy, you'd never get far as a writer. Any *other* ideas?"

Stung by his criticism, I replied, "Well, I suppose I could... *teach*."

"Higgy, teaching is the last refuge for failures. Surely, you've heard the old saying, 'Those who can, *do*; those who can't, *teach*'? Of course, the *ultimate* last refuge for failures is this: Those who can't *teach* become literary agents."

That was a novel idea. "A literary agent?" I said. "What do *they* do?"

"Not much at all," he replied. "Which is the beauty of that profession."

He sipped his drink and, with great effort, reached over the enormous mountain of his belly toward a bowl of mixed nuts. He scooped up a handful and dropped them into his mouth.

"A literary agent works a couple of hours a day...*at most*," he explained, chewing the nuts. "They take three-hour martini lunches. They travel occasionally to meet authors. All of their expenses come out of the author's share. *Yes*, the more I think of it, the better I like the idea. Being a literary agent is the perfect cover for your work with us at the CIA."

CHAPTER TEN

Which brings me to my early days as a *ten percenter*—a literary agent who takes ten percent of all his authors' earnings

As part of my CIA *legend*, I was the president of my very own company, the Sticky Fingers Literary Agency, and I naturally spent a lot of time in the publishing capital of the world, New York City, and especially at Elaine's, the East Side watering hole made famous by the likes of Michael Caine, Woody Allen, and Jackie Onassis. Elaine's was the Mecca for the city's big-name writers.

One night, Taitsie and I flew up from Washington to hang out at Elaine's. I intended to use Taitsie and her feminine charms as bait to hook a celebrity author for my agency. I told her it was important that she look her best for the occasion. Taitsie didn't disappoint. She wore a tan, tasseled rawhide miniskirt and a pair of brown suede five-inch-high platform heels. Not to be outdone by my gorgeous companion, I was decked out in a slouchy Armani sports jacket and a pair of silk willow-green slacks.

She made a grab for my crotch. "Not looking bad there, Bottom."

From the very beginning, Taitsie refused to call me Higgy, which she said she "hated." So she called me Theodore, which *I* hated. Taitsie found a compromise in calling me "Bottom." It came out like the sound you hear on the snare drums after a stand-up comic tells a joke—*bah-DUM!* I still get aroused every time I think about the way Taitsie drew out that word—*bah-DUM!*

My ardor was chilled on the Delta Shuttle to New York, when Taitsie finally told me the whole story of her affair with her father's old Princeton roommate, Richard "Rip" Hack.

"I'm a sculptor," she said. "I like to do nudes of women, especially black women, and my godfather Rip Hack saw my work and liked it. Rip sits on the board of the Museum of Modern Art and he was able to arrange a spot for me in a sculpture show at the museum. And, as they say, one thing led to another...."

I still found the idea revolting. "What did your mother think about her husband's old college roommate shagging her daughter?"

"You don't spare a girl, do you?" Taitsie said. "Well, the affair with Rip is over now, but while it lasted, my mother was naturally aghast. Like everybody else. Like you are probably, too."

"Aghast—*yes*—but not aghast at *you*," I said. "I'm aghast at Rip Hack for taking advantage of a vulnerable young girl."

"Bottom," Taitsie said, squeezing my hand, "I think this is the beginning of a beautiful friendship."

We hailed a taxi at LaGuardia Airport, and I told the driver to let us off on Second Avenue and Eighty-sixth Street, two blocks south of the famous yellow sign over Elaine's. At the corner, we passed a lighted phone booth. Inside stood a man dressed in cowboy boots, a pair of faded jeans, and a large black Stetson hat. Two things about him caught my attention: the slight dusting of white powder under his nose, and the fact that he was *urinating* in full view inside a lighted phone booth.

"You don't see *that* too often," I remarked to Taitsie.

"Thank God," she said, disgusted. "Whoever *he* is, I hope I never run into him."

I held open the door to Elaine's and we entered the noisy, smoke-filled saloon. The owner, Elaine Kaufman, came over to greet us. She took one look at the tassels hanging from Taitsie's rawhide miniskirt and said, "What's the matter, honey? Can't you afford a tailor for that hem?"

"Taitsie," I said, "meet Elaine."

Taitsie gave Elaine a friendly buss on the cheek, and Elaine broke into one of her surprisingly girlish smiles.

"Higgy," Elaine said, pointing at Taitsie, "I think this one's a keeper."

Elaine then led us to one of her coveted VIP tables against the wall in the front of her establishment. The table next to ours was occupied by a raucous group of heavy drinkers: Mike Lupica, the *New York Daily News* sports columnist; Pat O'Brien, the CBS sportscaster; and the writers Pete Hamill and Gay Talese.

"Come over and join us," Lupica said, addressing me but staring at Taitsie's long, slim legs.

"Sure…why not?" I said.

Gay Talese, ever the Old World gentleman, stood up and held a chair for Taitsie. As we resettled ourselves at the table, the door of Elaine's suddenly burst open and in stumbled the urinating phone-booth cowboy we had passed on Second Avenue.

"Hey, Don!" Lupica called to him.

The cowboy plopped down on the seat next to Taitsie's. I could hear her suck in her breath.

"Meet Don Imus…syndicated radio host, humorist, philanthropist, and equal opportunity addict," Lupica said.

Don Imus sniffled and rubbed his nose with the back of his hand.

"We've met—sort of," Taitsie said. "I thought that white mustache came from a jelly donut."

"I'm sorry," Imus said, turning to Taitsie, "but you have me at a disadvantage. I don't recall our having been introduced."

"We caught your act in the phone booth," Taitsie said. "*Relieving* yourself."

"Oh, *that*," Imus said, flashing a sheepish smile. "Believe me, that was the *least* offensive thing I did today. In any case, our formal introduction deserves to be memorialized by a drink!"

He summoned the waiter.

"A drink for the lady," he said, "and a round of drinks for *everyone* else in the joint!"

Lupica leaned over toward me. "In addition to a good shrink and a good accountant, Don needs a good *literary* agent," he said. "This is your big chance, Higgy. Go for it!"

"Well, Don…" I began.

"You can't call me *that*," he said. "Only my friends call me Don. And you aren't my friend."

"And only *his* friends call him Higgy," said Taitsie with just enough flirtiness to disarm the irascible Imus.

He took one long measure of her voluptuous legs. "Okay," he said, "you can call me Don if I can have your date's phone number."

I ignored this preposterous suggestion. Taitsie would no sooner go out with him than she would jump into bed with a pair of lesbians. Instead, I made, in my innocence of those days, an offer I was sure would charm him. "Don," I said, "if you let me represent you as your literary agent, I promise I'll read *every* draft…*every* paragraph …*everything* you write. And I'll help you become a best-selling author."

"Why would you bother to *read* any of my shit?" he asked.

I was surprised. "Because if I'm going to represent you I need to know *what* I'm representing."

"That's crazy, man," he said.

He was clearly stone drunk. I tried to get through to him by appealing to what I knew to be his soft spot. "Listen," I said, "don't you read the books and articles by the authors you interview on your radio show?"

"He can't even remember *who* he interviewed this morning!" said Pete Hamill.

"Higgy, let me tell you something," Imus said, ignoring Hamill. "You've got to change your entire approach as a literary agent. I mean it. You've got to adopt my theory of inverse proportion. The *less* work you do, the *more* successful you become. You've got to *stop* reading the manuscripts they send you. If you want to be a *really* successful agent, you've got to stop reading *altogether*. Just call up the book editors, make a submission, and within a week or so you'll have a contract. Believe me, Higgy, making money on ten percent commissions will be a snap."

Then he turned to Taitsie.

"So what's your telephone number, sweetheart?" he asked.

Taitsie smiled at him but didn't say anything.

"If you don't give it to me, I'll have my show's producer look it up," Imus said.

"Sorry, buster," Taitsie said, "but I'm unlisted."

Instead, she reached over and grabbed my hand. Holding it up like a winning prizefighter, she announced, "Him, I'm betting the house on him."

CHAPTER ELEVEN

In the spring of 1986, during one of my secret trips to the Middle East on behalf of the CIA, I sent Taitsie a telegram. It said: MARRY ME?

She replied: YOURS IS THE BEST OFFER I'VE HAD SO FAR THIS MORNING. SO THE ANSWER IS: LET'S DO IT!

We set a date for a summer wedding at the Provincetown Inn so that Taitsie's artsy friends on Cape Cod could attend. After the wedding cake was cut and the toasts were over, The Deuce took me aside.

"Higgy, Bill Casey needs a favor," he said.

"Sure, Dad."

"You and Taitsie are planning a two-week honeymoon in the Greek Islands, right? Bill has a proposition for you. He'll pay for your entire honeymoon—plane fare, the yacht, all of it—but he needs you to pop into Tripoli to see someone."

"Who?" I asked.

My father turned ultra casual, a sure sign I was in for trouble. "He wants you to represent President Reagan at a small ceremony just outside of Tripoli in honor of Libya's president, Muammar Khaddafi. When you meet the Colonel, hand him this box and tell him it's a gift from President Reagan."

Taitsie was thrilled with this little side trip. Of course, she didn't know my real purpose. She believed that my only business was the Sticky Fingers Literary Agency, which I ran out of an office attached to our house on M Street in Georgetown. The idea of a quickie trip to an exotic locale like Tripoli acted like an aphrodisiac on her imagination.

On the plane from Frankfurt, we joined the Mile High Club—twice. The first time, we did it in the lavatory, while a German stewardess pounded on the door shouting "*Sie müssen aufhören!*" "You must cease!" The second time was just before the breakfast service. We did it under a blanket using a position I had never even dreamed of before. Just as Taitsie reached orgasm, she cried out, "*Sie müssen aufhören!*" and we both cracked up. From then on, *Sie müssen aufhören!* was our secret signal when we wanted to do the two-backed beast.

The CIA station chief's wife picked us up at the airport and took us to the Al-Kabir Hotel. On the drive, Taitsie couldn't stop talking about the dark-skinned Libyan women and their clothes.

"Oh, Bottom, look at that *bui bui*! I'd love to sculpt that woman *nude*!"

I paid little attention to her fascination with Muslim women and their *bui buis*. My mind was on the assignment at hand. I was to attend a small Muslim ceremony, called an *al-Tasmyia*, where a child is officially given his or her name. In this particular case, the child was the daughter of Colonel Muammer Khaddafi, the Libyan strong man.

The Colonel, unlike the Ayatollah, did indeed live in a tent. Granted, *his* tent was twice as large as Barnum & Bailey's, and it had dozens of rooms and toilets with running water. But the colonel was, as my mother used to say about the people The Deuce dragged home for dinner, "an odd duck." He wore lipstick and makeup and his teeth were all fake and filled with gold. He was protected by forty gun-toting female bodyguards in khaki uniforms and red berets. He insisted that these women be both virgins and experts in hand-to-hand combat.

As instructed, I handed the box to Khaddafi, and passed on President Reagan's best wishes. The colonel opened the box and saw that it contained a gold necklace encrusted with diamonds that spelled out the Arabic words *assalamu-alaikum,* which translated as "Peace be upon you." I figured the present was for his twelve-year-old daughter, but he immediately draped it around his own neck and had one of his virgin bodyguard fasten the clasp.

Taitsie and I left the next day, bound for Athens and our cruise around the Greek Islands. But before we left Libya, she said, "Bottom, I have an idea. Let's do it camel-style."

"*Sie müssen aufhören!* I replied.

Later, while we were on the yacht *Daphne* off the Greek island of Santorini, I heard on the shortwave radio that the CIA station chief in Tripoli and an unidentified Libyan woman had been assassinated in the Al-Kabir Hotel. I immediately phoned The Deuce.

"What happened?" I asked.

"Do you remember that necklace you gave Khaddafi?"

"Of course," I said. "He was supposed to give it to his daughter, but he kept it for himself."

"Not exactly" The Deuce said. "The necklace contained a CIA-engineered homing device that was intended to guide our bombers to a target in Libya. We planned to retaliate for Khaddafi's terrorist bombings in Europe. But things didn't quite work out that way."

"How so?" I asked.

"Well," The Deuce said, "it seems that Khaddafi didn't like the way the gold in the necklace clashed with the gold fillings in his false teeth, so he gave the necklace to his daughter. She, in turn, gave it to her nanny, who in real life was an undercover agent working for the CIA. And the nanny turned over the necklace to our station chief in Libya, who should have checked it out, but instead *he* gave it to his Libyan mistress. And the damned thing acted as a guidance system for our bombers just when the station chief and his mistress were doing the nasty at the Al-Kabir Hotel...."

There was a long pause on the other end of the line and for a moment I thought I had lost my phone connection to The Deuce.

Then I heard him say: "To make a long story short, Higgy, we bombed ourselves*!*"

CHAPTER TWELVE

In 1990, I received a letter addressed to the Sticky Fingers Literary Agency from an aspiring author at Harvard University who was looking for a literary agent. He signed his name "President Barry Obama" and used the *Harvard Law Review* as his return address.

I made an appointment to see him and flew up to Boston. When I arrived at the offices of the *Harvard Law Review* just after six o'clock in the evening, I found the place a beehive of activity. Three male secretaries manned the phones, which were ringing constantly.

"Good evening, Senator Kennedy," one of the secretaries said into the phone. "Yes...yes he's in...just a moment." The secretary pressed an intercom button and said, "Mr. President, it's Senator Kennedy on line three for you."

Ten minutes passed, then fifteen. Finally, the secretary called over to me.

"The president will see you now," he said. "Please follow me."

The secretary led me down a hall to a polished wood door with a large brass knob. He knocked once and then opened the door.

"Mr. Higginbothem to see you, Mr. President."

The office was an exact replica of the Oval Office! Everything was exactly the same down to the last detail—the presidential desk; the sofa; two sitting chairs in front of a fireplace; the American flag; the red, white and blue rug with an embossed presidential seal; even the credenza behind the desk. Six framed photographs lined the credenza—five of them of presidents of the United States who had attended Harvard: John Adams, John Quincy Adams, Theodore Roosevelt, Franklin Roosevelt, and John F. Kennedy. The sixth portrait was of the young man sitting in the chair behind the desk: Barry Obama.

"Welcome," he said, getting up to greet me.

Barry Obama was a tall, rail-thin young man with a trim Afro haircut. He had an engaging smile that displayed a set of large white teeth. To my practiced fashion eye, he was the best-dressed graduate student I had ever seen. He was wearing a dark blue suit from the Hart Shaffner Marx "Gold Trumpeter Collection."

He placed his hand on my elbow and guided me over to the sofa. He took one of the chairs by the fireplace, leaned back and stretched his long legs out in front of him. He fished out a pack of Marlboros and a gold lighter from his inside jacket pocket.

"You mind?" he asked.

"No...go right ahead."

He took a long drag on the Marlboro and then said, "I'm writing my memoirs. I expect it to be a runaway bestseller. And I'm looking for an agent."

"Do you think you've had enough experience in life to fill the pages of a memoir?" I asked.

"There's nothing to worry about, Mr. Higginbothem," he said. "My staff here at the *Review* has already outlined and written the first draft. They tell me I'm the most fascinating person they've ever met. One of a kind. Peerless. Unrivaled. Nonpareil. The one and only. Notable. Incomparable."

"Allow me to play devil's advocate for a moment," I said, interrupting him. "Why would anyone shell out their hard-earned cash to buy a memoir from someone who isn't even thirty years old?"

"Because," he said, "I am... the *first*. The *first* African-American president of the *Harvard Law Review*. And I intend to be the *first* African-American president of the United States. I'm the one everybody's been waiting for."

Just then the phone on his desk rang. It wasn't a normal ring. It was *Ruffles and Flourishes*, the fanfare that is played for the president of the United States before *Hail to the Chief*.

Barry picked up the phone, listened for a moment, and then put down the receiver.

"My accountant needs a quick word with me," he explained.

There was a knock on the door and a harried-looking student entered the office.

"Barry…uh…Mr. President," he said. "The monthly budget figures just came in. All this furniture. The rug with the embossed presidential seal. The extra secretaries. The rented limo and the chauffeurs. You're going to bust the budget!"

"Hey," Barry said. "Don't sweat it. That's what budgets are *for.* To be busted!"

I didn't think so much about it then. I passed him up as an author, of course. Who in the world would ever want to read about someone with a weird name like Barack Obama? Yet even that first time I could tell he stood out from the crowd. Just why he stood out, I didn't know then. But I would soon have occasion to find out everything about him.

CHAPTER THIRTEEN

As the years passed, I learned to juggle my multiple personalities. In my guise as Personality Number One, I was the devoted husband, who kissed his wife goodbye in the morning and came home faithfully every night for *Sie müssen aufhören!* Then there was my Personality Number Two—the successful millionaire president of the Sticky Fingers Literary Agency, who revolutionized the publishing industry by refusing to read a word that my authors wrote. And finally there was Personality Number Three—the undercover CIA agent, who disappeared for weeks on end without explanation.

As far as I was concerned, Joanne Woodward in *The Three Faces of Eve* had nothing on me. But then one day my boss at the CIA, Whitney Nutwing, summoned me to his office and upset my cozy, carefully balanced multiple-personality-*dis*ordered life.

"Higgy," said Nutwing, "someone in President George Herbert Walker Bush's reelection campaign headquarters has been stealing classified State Department records. This person pulled the files on Bill Clinton, Bush's Democratic opponent, and stuffed them down his boxer underwear."

"How do you know he wasn't wearing jockeys?" I joked.

"Because when one of the State Department's female security guards saw the culprit leaving the building, she noticed a huge bulge in the front of his pants, and she said, "Did you stuff classified documents in your underpants or are you just glad to see me?' And the guy took off like a bat out of hell…out of *hell*… and some of the pages starting falling out of his boxer shorts and down the legs of his trousers and he left a trail…like Hansel and Gretel in the woods.…the woods to grandma's house. Except, when we followed the paper trail, it didn't lead to any *woods*. It led to the Bush reelection campaign headquarters… headquarters. And we figured out who the culprit was… the culprit."

"Who's that?" I asked.

"Poppy Bush's chief of staff and closest friend, James Baker," Nutwing said. "It seems that Jim Baker's got it into his head that Bill Clinton worked for the KGB when he was a Rhodes scholar at Oxford… a Rhodes scholar.…and traveled to Eastern Europe. If Jim Baker can prove that Bill Clinton cooperated with the KGB, it'll destroy Bill Clinton's chances of beating Poppy Bush at the polls in November."

"So what?" I said. "Doesn't the CIA *want* Poppy Bush to win? After all, Poppy Bush used to be the *director* of the CIA."

"I wish it was as simple as that, The-o-*dore*…"

"Call me Higgy."

"I mean, *Higgy*," Nutwing said. "You see, without knowing it, Jim Baker has stumbled upon one of the most closely guarded secrets of the Cold War."

Nutwing paused to let that sink in.

"Higgy," he went on, "what I'm about to tell you is so classified that only four thousand people in the national security community know about it. Plus Bob Woodward at the *Washington Post*. But that's *all*. When Bill Clinton was at Oxford... at Oxford...he cut a secret deal with the CIA to infiltrate the anti-Vietnam War movement. Bill Clinton was—and, in fact, Bill Clinton still *is*—an agent for the agency!"

"Do you mean to *say* that the man running on the Democratic ticket for president is an agent for the agency!" I asked.

"Yes, an agent for the agency."

"Do you mean to *say* that the man running for president sold out his friends in the anti-war movement?" I asked.

"In a heartbeat," Nutwing confirmed.

"Do you mean to *say*... What *do* you mean to say?"

"That's how Bill Clinton beat the draft," Nutwing said, raising his finger like a detective announcing a great deduction. "In return for his cooperation, the CIA kept him out of the army. But nobody can ever know about this, Higgy. If Bill Clinton is elected president, we'll have an agent for the agency—one of our very *own*— sitting in the White House...in the White House, *Higgy*. Can you imagine *that*?"

"No, I can't," I said. "The words 'president' and 'Clinton' don't parse."

"Higgy," Nutwing said, "I'm sending you to London to head off Jim Baker and anyone else who might dig up the truth about Bill Clinton and the CIA. Godspeed. And remember what that great rocketeer Wernher von Braun said."

"What's that?" I asked, pretending I hadn't heard Whitney Nutwing quote Wernher von Braun before.

"It was toward the end of World War II," Nutwing said, "and Von Braun said: *'Bomb the shit out of London and kill all those Limey bastards!'* "

CHAPTER FOURTEEN

The next day, I checked into the Hotel Cavendish London, which was a short walk from my favorite Savile Row tailor, Alta Cocka & Shmuley. At the reception desk, who should I run into but the one man in the whole world who put the fear of God in the heart of every CIA agent—Russia's legendary spymaster, Yurik Maligin.

Maligin had risen to his exalted rank in the old KGB, which recently had been rechristened the *Federal'naya sluzhba bezopasnosti Rossiyskoy Federatsii*—the Federal Security Service, or FSB—to make it sound more sibilantly friendly to Western ears. *Eff-esss-be* r-r-rolled off the tongue. But according to the CIA's psychological profilers at Langley, Maligin was a psychopath. He could be charming, humorous and culturally refined. But beneath that pleasant exterior was a savage Cossack. He had a mansion in the Black Sea port city of Sevastopol, where he reportedly employed a team of sadistic Crimean Tatar hunchbacks who tortured anyone who got in his way.

For a villain, Maligin turned out to be a lot *shorter* than I expected. That wasn't the only thing about Maligin that took me by surprise. In movies, a mangy dog always slinks away when the villain appears. But Maligin was carrying a Basset Hound under each arm, and those dogs were licking every square inch of his villainous face.

"Comrade Higgy," Maligin said. "I recognized you instantly from your photos in our FSB file. I've heard a lot about you."

"All *not* good, I hope."

"Absolutely not," he said, smiling. "I've heard the most *terrible* things about you. *Wonderful* terrible things! And that only makes me want to know you better. Let me buy you a drink. We can discuss why the two best spies in America and Russia happen to be here in London at exactly the same time."

I wanted to let him know that I was no chump. "I think we both know why," I sneered.

"Yes," Maligin said. "Isn't it ironic? The CIA, the Bushies, and the FSB—all running after the same information about Bill Clinton."

"But only *I* know where to look."

"Don't be so sure," Maligin said. "I have the nose of a Basset Hound."

He glanced down at the Bassett Hounds under his arms.

"Meet Gulag and Archipelago," he said, introducing his dogs.

While I petted them, Maligin looked around as though he just remembered he had lost something.

"Where is that fucking assistant of mine, that Charnofsky," he muttered. "Oh, there you are, you dumb retard. Get your fat ass over here!"

A bedraggled Russian with a head of patchy hair sidled up to Maligin. This was obviously Maligin's assistant Charnofsky. He had a pair of droopy, sad eyes that gave him the look of a Basset Hound.

"Take Gulag and Archipelago outside" Maligin ordered Charnofsky. "They need to piss and poop."

"But I don't have any more poopie bags," Charnofsky said.

"Then pick up the mess with your bare hands," Maligin said.

Before Maligin could give Charnofsky a more graphic description of how to clean up after Gulag and Archipelago, I bid him farewell and went to my room on the sixth floor of the Hotel Cavendish London.

The bellhop deposited my steamer trunk and several other suitcases, and then left. As soon as the door clicked shut behind him, I heard a woman's voice calling from the bathroom.

"Higgy, Higgy… I'm in here!"

Waiting for me in the bathtub, covered in pink bubbles, was the most beautiful redhead I had ever laid eyes on. Her breasts floated above the bubbles. She smiled at me as she ran a sponge over her long, thin, shapely legs.

"Care to join me?" she asked.

I was instantly on guard. I knew she was trying to seduce me. "I had a bath this morning," I said. "I'm still clean."

“Then hand me a large bath towel,” she said, emerging naked from the pink bubbles.

I gave her the towel and turned away—but not before catching a ravenous eyeful. That was only common courtesy.

“The least you can do is dry my back,” she said.

I began drying her back in an offhand way so that she wouldn’t think I enjoyed it.

“I know why you’re here in London,” she said, squirming under my touch and rubbing her rear end into my crotch.

“You’re getting me wet,” I said.

“That’s the idea,” she said.

“Not that kind of wet,” I said. “I mean you’re getting water all over my pants.”

She gave me a dirty look. “Sorry,” she said. “Anyway, I know that you’ve come here to track down Jean Sejna, the only person other than Bill Clinton himself who knows the whole story of his involvement with the CIA.”

“Who are *you*?” I asked as I started working on her breasts—drying her breasts.

“I’m Jean Sejna’s daughter, Masha,” she said. “My mother was a Czech intelligence agent working for the KGB who used her considerable sexual skills—and an unlimited supply of drugs—to coax young Bill Clinton into her bed. But recruiting him to the Communist side proved to be considerably more difficult than she had expected.”

“Why was that?” I said. “Was it because Bill Clinton was, in his heart of hearts, an American patriot?”

"Not at all," Masha said. "It was because Bill Clinton wanted to dodge the draft. And the KGB couldn't help him out on *that* score. Only your CIA could."

That sounded like typical presidential timber. "Where's your mother now?"

"Dead," she said. "Tortured to death by Yurik Maligin's team of sadistic Crimean Tatar hunchbacks in Sebastopol."

"I hope she didn't spill the beans about Bill Clinton before she died," I said. "The CIA doesn't want that information to fall into the hands of the FSB."

"No," Masha Sejna said, "my mother died with her lips sealed. By the way, you can stop rubbing my crotch now. I think it's dry."

"Oh, of course." Flinging the towel into the bathtub, I followed her out into the bedroom. She switched on the hotel radio and found a station that was playing Bohemian polkas. Then she danced for me in the nude. Soon, I was on my feet, dancing along with her. Before I knew it we were on her bed and Masha was crying out in pleasure, *Musíe prestat!* Which is Czech for "You must cease!"

I eventually convinced Masha Sejna to stop shrieking and put on some clothes. Then I explained that if she, too, fell into the hands of Yurik Maligin, her life wouldn't be worth a plug Czech koruna. We agreed that I would arrange a new identity for her, deposit a great deal of money in a Lichtenstein bank account, and send her to an undisclosed location in America.

Thanks to my quickie—I mean, quick—attention to Masha, the Bill Clinton Matter was put to rest. Jim Baker and the Bushies were never the wiser. And I had the satisfaction of knowing that I had outwitted Yurik Maligin.

Before I left London, he and I met again, this time for high tea at Brown's Hotel. We clinked teacups, and I said:

"Too bad you lost, Yurik."

"There's always a next time, my dear Higgy," Maligin told me with a malicious gleam in his eye. "And I will do *everything* in my power to make sure *I* win. I will stop at *nothing!*"

For the first time since I had met him, I believed Yurik Maligin was telling the truth. We *were* fated to meet another day and engage in a life-and-death struggle for supremacy. Little did I know that our struggle would be over a prepuce—the retractable roll of skin covering the end of the penis that is customarily referred to as the foreskin.

BOOK TWO

CHAPTER FIFTEEN

Early one morning in the summer of 2004, I found a coded message in disappearing caffeine ink floating in my Starbucks Frappuccino. I took it back to my house on M Street and decoded it. My boss at the CIA, Whitney Nutwing, had written:

> Meet me at 12 noon in the bowels of the National Museum of Health and Medicine behind the Walter Reed Army Medical Center. Tell no one. WN

I got into my 1964 Bentley S3 Continental "Chinese Eye" and roared over to the museum, a sprawling cabinet of curiosities that housed five thousand skeletal specimens and eight thousand preserved organs. I had perused the exhibits a dozen times with keen curiosity, wanting to know every single aspect of my deadly craft.

Nutwing was waiting for me in the shadows of the museum basement, his arm outstretched, his palm warm and moist. As we shook hands, I noticed he had put on more weight; he tipped the scales at 400 pounds. He was now so obese that he had to support himself with a pair of elaborately carved, silver-tipped *bastone da passegio,* Italian walking sticks. He leaned forward at a forty-five-degree angle, all his weight on the thick wooden sticks. Dangling from his neck, like an equine hay bag, was a white paper bag, from which he extracted a gooey piece of pastry.

"Ah, my dear The-o-*dore!*" he wheezed in his inimitable husky faux-British accent. "Isn't this museum wonderful ... wonderful. Just look at that display! Marvelous...*marvelous!*"

He was pointing at a lit glass cylinder that contained the brain and skeleton of President Garfield's assassin. Next to that specimen was a jar displaying a piece of John Wilkes Booth's spine.

"Want one?" Nutwing asked.

For a second I thought he was referring to the mummified remains. But then I realized he was offering me something from the white paper bag around his neck. Inside were a dozen large cinnamon rolls, topped with caramel and pecans, which Nutwing had purchased at a local Cinnabon kiosk.

"No thanks," I said.

He hobbled over to another glass display case. "I just love *this* one," he said. "Just *love...*"

He reached into the white paper bag and grabbed another cinnamon roll and stuffed it into his mouth. He licked his fingers and pointed to the hairball of a twelve-year-old girl who had compulsively eaten her own hair and died in the process.

"Delicious, isn't it?"

I wasn't sure whether he was referring to the cinnamon roll or the hairball.

"The-o-*dore*," he said after he managed to swallow yet another cinnamon roll, "the CIA is quite certain that George W. Bush will defeat John Kerry and be re-elected president this November. You know we always wanted that boy to be president. Ever since his father was director of the CIA, we had our eyes on George W., because we knew he could be controlled by us. We took an inarticulate, malleable, and not-very-bright boy, the black sheep of the Bush Family—a guy who snorted cocaine at Camp David when his father was president—and we made that boy *our* President."

Nutwing dug into the bag of cinnamon rolls.

"The-o-*dore*..." he went on.

"Call me Higgy," I said.

"Now, *Higgy*, the CIA has had an off-the-books domestic operation for decades, in which we keep tabs on our most ambitious presidential hopefuls. We compile dossiers on all of them, we infiltrate their staffs, we bug their homes and cars and offices, and we even bug their mistresses' or boyfriends' homes... their *homes*. We do this in order to defend ourselves from the miscreant, publicity-seeking politician who might become president of the United States and get it into his head to play games with our budget."

He was winded by his long monologue and he paused for a moment to catch his breath.

"In short," he said at last, "our job is to get *our* guy—Democrat or Republican—into the White House. And once he's there, to make sure he *stays* on the straight and narrow...yes, you heard me—the straight and narrow."

I knew that federal law expressly prohibited the CIA from operating *inside* the United States. But I also knew enough to know that the Persian philosopher Sara Truth wouldn't consider it *constructive* for me to point out that inconvenient truth to Nutwing.

He handed me a copy of that morning's *Boston Globe*. "Did you see this?"

I recognized the figure staring back at me from the front page right away. It was a photograph of Barack Obama. These days he was a state senator from Illinois. He had given the keynote address the previous night at the Democratic National Convention in Boston. The Democrats had nominated the ticket of John Kerry and John Edwards. But judging by the size and play of Barack Obama's photo, *his* performance had stolen the show from the two Johns. Why was I not surprised?

"Fourteen years ago, The-o-*dore*...I mean Higgy...you met this guy Obama when he was president of the *Harvard Law Review*," Nutwing reminded me. "All our indicators show that four years from now, in 2008, he's going to make a run for *president* of the United States. And we think he's got a good chance of winning."

"You've got to be kidding," I said.

"I want you to take a good look at this photo of Obama on the front page. Who do you see standing right behind him?"

I inspected the photo again. "Holy Toledo! Is *that* who I *think* it is?"

"Yes," said Nutwing. "That's Yurik Maligin, the legendary spymaster of the FSB."

I tried to recall what Maligin had told me years ago in London when I had outwitted him on the Bill Clinton case. We had met for high tea at Brown's and Maligin had threatened me.... How had he put it? All at once, I remember his exact words:

"There's always a next time, my dear Higgy. And I will do everything in my power to make sure I win. I will stop at nothing!"

"Higgy," Nutwing said, "I want you to do a complete workup on Barack Obama before *Maligin* gets the goods on him. Everything about Obama's past...his personal life...his habits... girls...boys...drugs...where he buys those neat neckties. You'll be in a race against the legendary spymaster Yurik Maligin. But your team will be given the highest classification; it will be the most secret directorate in the CIA. It's even going to be given a very special name. It will be called...are you ready for this?... *The Tchaikovsky Circle.*"

From the intense pleasure he derived from the name, I had no doubt who had originally thought it up.

"That sounds sibilantly *Communist*," I said.

He wagged a stubby finger at me. "The *original* Tchaikovsky Circle was a nineteenth-century secret Russian society that fought to reverse Russia's moral decay... yes, *moral* decay. *Our* Tchaikovsky Circle will have a similar goal: fighting the downhill slide in America's *moral* values." I knew he considered me slow, and he added pointedly, "Pyotr Illyich Tchaikovsky was a composer, not a Commie. He died long before the Communists came to power in Russia."

As we parted company, I didn't have the heart to tell Whitney Nutwing that the *original* Tchaikovsky Circle wasn't named after the famous composer; it was named after *Nikolai* Tchaikovsky, a flaming radical who fought on the side of the Communists during the Russian Revolution.

Whitney Nutwing had named my new unit—the CIA's most *secret* directorate—after a Communist hero.

CHAPTER SIXTEEN

One week to the day after Whitney Nutwing created The Tchaikovsky Circle, I found myself standing at the luggage carousel in Chicago's O'Hare Airport. Chicago was ground zero in Barack Obama's political career.

I was traveling, as was my custom, with a gigantic Louis Vuitton wardrobe trunk that accommodated three suits, a tuxedo, a blue blazer, two pairs of slacks, workout clothes, sneakers, several pairs of shoes, plus shirts, sweaters, and accessories. It took two brawny porters to wrestle the monster into a taxi. Seeing them grunt and strain made me chuckle. No effort in the name of fashion was too great.

I told the driver to take me to The Townhouse at 107 East Oak Street, and asked him to wait for me there. This was the location of Paul Stuart, my favorite men's store. I bought a half dozen pairs of jockey undershorts, one size too small. I always remembered my father's sage advice: "There's nothing like feeling firmly supported when you begin a tough new assignment."

My next stop was the Ambassador East, a luxury hotel on Lake Michigan. A diminutive bellhop who looked as old as the hotel itself (it was built in 1926) escorted me to a suite on a high floor. He was so decrepit that he could barely manage to open the curtains.

"Mister," he said in a wheezy voice, "I don't know who you are, but you sure must be major league to rate this suite. When Old Joe Kennedy came to Chicago, he met right here, in this very room, with Sam Giancana, the boss of bosses of the Chicago Outfit. This is where Old Joe and Sam hatched their scheme to get Jack Kennedy elected president back in 1960."

"I'm impressed," I said.

And I *was* impressed. Until then I had never thought of myself as being in the same business as Joseph P. Kennedy—the making of a president.

"And you see that red stain on the carpet?" the old bellhop continued, pointing to a spot near my feet. "That's from the 1957 murder of Teddy Roe, a South Side bookmaker who refused to pay Sam Giancana the going street tax. Giancana had Teddy Roe rubbed out right where you're standing." He paused, then added: "Believe me, Mister, Chicago's *still* that kind of a town."

If he thought he was putting the fear of God into me, he didn't know the kind of man he was dealing with.

That evening, instead of eating downstairs in the dining room, I slipped on a pair of Derek Rose brushed Egyptian cotton striped pajamas and ordered room service: lobster bisque, fresh trout *a la meunière*, puré of squash, *haricot vert almondine*, and, for desert, *profiteroles au chocolat* and a double espresso. Caffeine never kept me up at night. I always slept like a baby—a fact that I attributed to my untroubled conscience.

The next morning, feeling refreshed and with my loins appropriately girded, I strolled out of the Ambassador East Hotel lobby and walked a few blocks to a nondescript office building near the Sears Tower. I took the elevator to the eighth floor and entered through a door with a brass nameplate that said MITT.

In case anybody asked, MITT stood for the Midwestern Institute for Traditional Thinking. The CIA had established these think tanks and non-profit front organizations all over the country. (It's only fair to point out that the CIA created MITT long before Mitt Romney dropped his real first name, because he didn't think that an elder in the Mormon Church named Willard could get elected president.)

Waiting for me in the conference room, drinking from a can of Coca-Cola, was Russ Slanover, a chip head tech wiz with a mop of flaming red hair and a matching beard. Russ and I had worked together on several investigations. He could go on the Internet where no man had ever gone before. No website, no account, no firewall was off limits to Russ Slanover.

"Russ," I said, "I'm going to level with you. I met this guy Obama fourteen years ago, and never in my wildest dreams did I believe that a half-black, half-white man with a Muslim middle name…a man who's an obscure member of the Illinois state senate... never did I dream…. You tell me, what's the chance of somebody like that becoming president of the United States? Absolute *zero*, right?"

"Actually," Russ replied, extracting another can of Coke from his six-pack, "*absolute zero* can't be reached artificially because it's impossible to decouple a system fully from the rest of the universe."

"Yes," I said, "but—"

"So," Russ continued, popping open the can and taking a long swig of Coke, "if Obama doesn't have a chance of becoming president, why did Whitney Nutwing send you here? According to Moore's Paradox—which, as you know, is named after G. E Moore, one of the founders of the analytic tradition in philosophy—Nutwing must have thought about the relation of assertion and belief when it comes to Obama."

I was still trying to figure out what the heck the relation between assertion and belief could possibly be as I said, "I think this Barack Obama thing is another of Whitney Nutwing's wild goose chases. They don't call him 'Nutwing' for nothing."

"Of course they don't," Russ said. "They call him that because *that's* his name."

I let that pass. "So, have you been in contact with Vangie Roll yet?"

For all our past successes, Russ Slanover and I didn't know Shinola about Chicago. We needed to recruit a local expert to the Tchaikovsky Circle. I put in a phone call to the CIA's best deep-cover asset in the Windy City—Vangie Roll, a single black professional woman with both a law degree and a real estate license, who lived with Elvira, her eighty-one-year-old wheelchair-bound mother.

The phone was answered on the first ring.

"Vangie?" I said into the receiver. "Vangie *Roll*?"

"No, this ain't Vangie," said the voice on the other end. "Who's callin'?"

"Tell her it's Higgy."

"Tell her yourself, honky. This is Vangie's mother, Elvira."

"Elvira," I said, "how *are* you?"

I hadn't spoken to Elvira in quite a while, and I could hear her labored breathing over the phone line. She had been a heavy smoker, and suffered from an advanced case of emphysema. All her life, Elvira had been a very active woman. Back in the late 1940s, she had become the first black woman to be admitted to the Illinois Bar Association. And she had worked hand in glove with Thurgood Marshall during the civil rights movement in the 1960s. I imagined that it was hard for her to be sidelined in her old age.

"Higgy," Elvira asked, "do you know what's white and twelve inches long?"

"No," I said, glancing downward idly. "What?"

"Nothin'."

Elvira broke into one of her deep, cigarette-smoker cackles, which quickly turned into a coughing jag. When she had recovered, she said:

"Why haven't you called Vangie? She's been *pining* away for you."

"I'm sure Vangie's got plenty of male suitors," I said.

"Yeah, but you're still the one and only, Higgy. You're the one she's been waitin' for. Hang on, here she is."

"Sorry about Mom's non-P.C. sense of humor," Vangie said when she came on the phone.

"No problemo."

"Oh, Higgy," Vangie said rapturously, "it's been so long that I almost forgot how much I loved to hear your voice. Say something—say *any*thing..."

"Vangie," I said, ignoring her request, "I need to see you. I'm at the Midwestern Institute for Traditional Thinking."

"I'll be there in twenty."

Sure enough, twenty minutes later Vangie Roll strode into the MITT conference room. She was a tall woman, well over six feet, and she was dressed in a green pantsuit with a short fitted jacket that accentuated her toned figure.

Vangie had been a star on the University of Tennessee's championship women's basketball team, and then played in a professional women's league in Eastern Europe, which is where the CIA recruited her. She was still involved in an amateur basketball league at the University of Chicago on weekends. Because she had an athlete's build and a face filled with humor and kindness, people often underestimated her intelligence. But Vangie Roll was as sharp as they came. She was, hands down, the best agent I'd ever worked with.

She gave me a buss on the cheek and lingered there long enough for me to feel the warm breath on my ear and smell the rich, woody, Oriental scent of Chanel *Cuir de Russie* ("Russia Leather") *Parfum*, which went for $700 an ounce.

"Where'd you get that outfit?" Vangie asked as soon as we had settled into our chairs.

I was wearing a summer-weight tan gabardine suit with a dark blue, modified spread-collar shirt, and a paisley tie.

"Paul Stuart," I said. "Don't you like it?"

"Uh-uh," she said, shaking her head. "As they say where I come from, 'You so square don't make me shank you.' "

"But I *am* square," I said.

"Not to *me*, you're not," she said. "To me, you're the most attractive man in the world. You'd look great in Dolce and Gabbana."

"Well, as long as we're talking about what we're wearing and *not* wearing," I said, "why aren't you wearing the engagement ring your fiancé gave you?"

She looked like she didn't want to tell me. "He flew the coop with another bird."

"He broke his engagement with you?" I asked. "How many does that make?"

"I've lost count," she lamented. "Mom's on my case about men all the time. She says the problem is that my heart belongs to the *one* man who isn't *interested* in me. I'm sure you know who I'm referring to...*Higgy.* "

"Yeah...right," I said. "So, uh, where does Barack Obama buy *his* suits?"

"Right here in Chicago—at Dillard's," Vangie said. "He gets made-to-measure Hart Schaffner Marx."

"Any relation to Karl?" I asked cheerfully.

"No such luck," Vangie said. "Obama buys Hart Schaffner Marx's 'Gold Trumpeter Collection.' Those suits go for $3,200 a pop."

I didn't appreciate the competition. "Where does he get that kind of money?"

"Higgy, you have no idea who you're dealing with," Vangie said.

"What do you mean?"

"I mean, you have no idea what Team Obama has going for them here in Chicago. This is Obama's first run for the United States Senate and, I tell you, he's going to win without breaking a sweat. The word on the street is that he's already planning his 2008 presidential campaign." She leaned a little closer to me. "Obama is the toughest, smartest, meanest political operator I ever saw. I'm telling you, Higgy, these Obama folks'll stop at nothing."

I suddenly recalled what the diminutive bellhop at the Ambassador East Hotel had told me:

"Mister, Chicago's still that kind of a town."

CHAPTER SEVENTEEN

A few days after my meetings with Russ Slanover and Vangie Roll, my phone rang at the Midwestern Institute for Traditional Thinking. I immediately recognized the ex-smoker's leathery voice as belonging to Vangie's disabled old mother, Elvira.

Vangie often let her mother dial her calls. It made Elvira, who used to be on a first-name basis with governors and Supreme Court justices, feel useful. But in this instance, most of what Elvira had to say was drowned out by music playing in the background.

"Elvira," I shouted into the receiver. "I can't hear you. Turn down the volume. What *is* that?"

"That's Ella Fitzgerald," she said. "I always knew you had Van Gogh's ear for music.... Hold on. Here's Vangie.

When Vangie came on the phone, she sounded breathless with excitement.

"Higgy, you aren't going to believe what happened to me today," she began. "Remember how I told you that I play in an amateur basketball league on weekends at the Ratner Center at the University of Chicago? Well, I was down there this morning, and who do you think I ran into in the gym? Our friend Barack Obama."

"Did you have a chance to talk to him?" I asked.

"Better than that," Vangie said. "The Ratner Center has three basketball courts, side by side, and when I saw Obama walk onto the far court with a group of players, I figured, hey, this is my big chance to get to know this guy. So I ditched my regular league game, and changed my uniform. I got into a tight-fitting black Nike tank top, which highlights my long arms, and a pair of matching skintight Under Armour bicycle pants, which accentuate my derriere. Do you dig me?"

"I follow you, Vangie," I said. "I can *picture* it. Go on."

"Well," she said, "I started working on my jump shot on the court right next to Obama's court. Which gave me the opportunity to keep an eye on him. The first thing I noticed was how *he* was the center of attention among all those big tall guys—some of them former college hoop stars, and some of them pros. They all gave Obama a man-hug, and then started a loud trash-talking exercise designed to endear themselves to Mr. Big Shot.

"I pretended I didn't notice any of this. I fired a long three-pointer, and heard the woosh of a 'just net' field goal. You know, Higgy, when I'm on the basketball court, I forget all my worries about my mother's health and things… and how you keep ignoring me…and breaking my heart.…"

"Vangie, please stick to the story," I said.

"It's like I was back playing basketball at Tennessee or in Moscow," she said. "Anyway, while I'm working on my jump shot, Obama's looking at his watch and talking into his cell phone. He looks really annoyed. And I figured out why. There were only five players, including Obama. He was one short to play three-on-three. He was waiting for somebody who hadn't showed up.

"I thought to myself, *Vangie Roll, this is your big chance. Don't blow it.* So I began a drill that I perfected in college: dribbling with alternative hands while running tight figure eights until I'm on the left side of the hoop. I then do a reverse lay-up, grab my own rebound, and repeat the drill in reverse. Believe me, I can do this exercise blindfolded without ever missing a dribble or a shot. Not to be arrogant about it, but few men in that gym could come close to doing what I was doing. An' dat'sda truth."

"I believe you," I said.

"After a dozen repetitions," she went on, "I was sweating and short of breath, so I stopped and grabbed a bottle of lemon flavored Gatorade. And as I gulped the drink, I purposely bent over and toweled the sweat off my sneakers. And just as I expected, I heard a voice saying, 'Excuse me.' And I knew who it was without looking up.

"I turned around and there, not three feet from me, was our mark, Barack Hussein Obama, with a big smile on his face. I noticed him give me a quick once-over, from my face all the way down to my toes and back up. He seemed particularly focused on my arms. Go figure that.

"He says to me, 'I hate to bother you, but I saw you practicing by yourself, and you look pretty good, and we're one player short....we have less than an hour left before I have to go change for a fundraiser. How would you like to play a little three-on-three with us?'

"And I say, 'Why not? Let me grab my stuff and I'll be right over.'

"But before I could pick up my gym bag, Obama's got it, and he's walking with me over to *his* court. Higgy, I have to admit his manners are impeccable, and he has a light, flirty way about him. The other players stopped as we arrived. They looked jealous at the ease with which he had picked me up."

I was feeling a little of that jealousy myself. "How did the game go?" I snapped.

"Great. Obama divided the six players into two teams," Vangie said, "and I ended up on the other team, and was assigned the task of guarding him. As a basketball player, he was fluid and smart; he ran his team as a point guard. He's not particularly fast, but he still moved well enough, and his jump shot was pretty steady.

"A couple of times, I decided to guard him aggressively. I used my long arms, and held my hands in front of his eyes to make it more difficult for him to measure the range of his shot. When I did that, he got flustered. But he remained polite, even when jive-talking to the other players on my team."

She paused, trying to add up her assessment of him. "One thing I saw right away was his ability to talk ghetto to the black players —'Yo game is phat, bro'—but talk preppy to the white guys—'Excuse me…so sorry….' Now, that's something I'd never encountered on the court before. That's an art, especially for an aspiring politician with national ambitions. And I wondered where he learned to switch it on and off like that."

She was admiring him entirely too much for my taste. It sounded like she had fallen in love with the man. "Go on," I said irritably.

"You know, Higgy, in pickup basketball, everybody's constantly calling fouls on the other team, and you can get into pretty heated arguments over these calls. But not Obama. He just laughed at these petty arguments. He even called a couple of fouls on himself —also something I had *never* seen on the court before. He would just stop the game, mutter, 'My bad,' and toss the ball to the other team. This impressed me.

"With just a few minutes left in the game, the intensity picked up, and Obama reverted to his favorite move: a drive to the hoop, a quick stop and then a sudden jump shot. By that time I knew it was coming, and I used my long arms to stuff the ball just as it came out of his left hand. The ball rolled away, and one of my teammates picked it up, scooted unopposed down the court, and jammed it into the basket for the winning score.

"Everybody was laughing at Obama. 'My oh my, she bitch-slapped you, man!' I laughed along with them. The game ended with handshakes all around and the players grabbed their towels and bags. But Obama hung back.

" 'You wanna sit for a sec?' he asked me.

" 'Sure,' I said."

I interrupted. "Of course, all he wanted to do was sit. Sure, I buy that, all the way."

She ignored my comment, then went on. "We walked over to the bleachers, and climbed up a couple of rows and sat down. Obama leaned back against the seat behind him, his long, lean legs stretched out in front of him.

"He said, 'You mind?' and he fished out a pack of Marlboro Lites and a matchbook from his bag.

" I said, 'No...go right ahead. Your wind was good in the game. Smoking doesn't bother you? '

"He laughed and said, 'It bothers me at home, I'll tell you that. My wife Michelle won't let me smoke in the house. So I have to sneak outside.'

"I wasn't sure if there was a double meaning in that comment, but if there was, he kept it pretty well hidden. He took a long drag on the Marlboro and then said, 'I'm running for the United States Senate, and I'm trying to shape up for a big fundraiser we're having soon. It's a basketball game featuring a bunch of NBA players. I hope I can hold my own.'"

"Oh, he'll do just fine," I remarked. "He'll just get run over by them."

"You know," she said, "what's funny is I could tell he was in love with the vertical pronoun. It was, *I* this, *I* that—all the time. His favorite topic was himself.

"I told him not to worry. I said, 'Oh, you got some game. Maybe not Division One level...but you can hold your own.'

"He was pleased by my praise, but he didn't return the compliment, even though he had to know I could run circles around him on the court. He didn't say anything about my playing. So I said, 'I played at Tennessee and then two years in the pro league in Moscow.'

"He didn't show the slightest interest in my basketball exploits. But he did seem mesmerized by my arms. I was still perspiring, and the veins in my arms were popping with engorged blood, and my biceps were defined and taut. Higgy, I've always been proud of my arms, but I've never seen a man so fascinated by a woman's arms.

"I decided to take advantage of his attraction to my blessed arms and ask him about something I'd seen in the *Sun-Times*."

'I read what your opponent in the United States Senate race, Alan Keyes, said about you yesterday. He claims you weren't even born in the United States. He says you were born in Mombasa, in Kenya.'

"For a fleeting moment—less than a nanosecond, but I caught it—a strange look came across his face. That look was filled with a combination of fright and evasion. Then he caught himself and, as if on cue, he gave me a wide smile and a dismissive shrug of his shoulders. But still, he stood right up, stamped out his cigarette butt, and said, 'You from around here?'"

'Hyde Park,' I said. 'Grew up there and still live there.'

"But he wasn't listening. I was no longer of any use to him. Instead, he packed up his things and grabbed his BlackBerry. He started checking his emails, paying no attention to me. So I got up, too, and waved good-bye, and walked out the door. I came straight home and called you on our secure line."

"That's terrific work, Vangie," I said. "Tell me, now that you've spent an hour or so with this guy, what's your professional evaluation?"

"Higgy," she said, "I think it would be a major mistake to write Obama off as just another narcissistic politician. Sure, he's totally obsessed with himself, and sees everything through a projection of himself. But he has two assets that make him different from your run-of-the-mill self-absorbed pol."

"What's that?"

"First off, he's what people where I come from call 'tight.' Meaning, he's sharp and smart and clever as hell, and a real cool customer."

"I can handle that," I said.

"But that's not the main thing that makes him different," Vangie continued in a more conspiratorial tone. "I told you, when we were sitting in the stands, I brought up the rumor being floated by Alan Keyes that Obama wasn't born in the United States. That he was born in Kenya?"

I started to get more interested. "Yeah?"

"And a look came over his face. Just for a fleeting moment. But I'm telling you this, Higgy. There's something there. There's *definitely* something there."

"What kind of something?"

Vangie took a moment before answering me.

"Higgy, for that one brief moment, I believe I saw deep into Barack Obama's soul. There's *something* about his birth. His official biography says he was born in Honolulu. But think about this: *if* he wasn't born in Honolulu—*if*, say, he was born in Kenya—*if* that's true, then he's not an American citizen, and he can't be elected president...."

I could hear her clap her hands and I wanted to join her. This was perfect. An overseas sleuthing job. Just the sort of job for a globe-trotting spy like moi.

CHAPTER EIGHTEEN

Once back in Washington, I wasted no time in setting up a meeting with Whitney Nutwing at his CIA safe house on Tracy Place.

"The Tchaikovsky Circle has hit pay dirt," I told him, blithely disregarding all the *ifs* surrounding the mystery of Barack Obama's birth—as well as the menacing meat hooks swinging from the ceiling. "It looks like our boy Obama might have been born in Kenya."

"Well, then, what are you waiting for?" Nutwing said, his hands on his commodious hips. "Start packing for the Dark Continent."

With the prospect of spending several weeks in Africa, I had an excuse to go on one of my clothes-buying sprees—all charged, of course, to the CIA. I bought three custom-fitted lightweight poplin suits; two African-style safari outfits; a new double-breasted white dinner jacket that made me look like Bogie in Rick's Café; a dozen lightweight Egyptian broadcloth cotton shirts; a new set of ties; and assorted sundries, such as hiking clothes and boots, a brand-new pair of Zeiss binoculars, two sun-reflective hats from Orvis, and two spray-bottles of DEET insect repellant.

As I was loading all of this stuff into my gigantic Louis Vuitton steamer wardrobe trunk, I heard Taitsie come down the stairs from her sculpture studio and say goodbye to her artist's models—two tall, gorgeous African-American women with to-die-for bodies. The front door closed and Taitsie made her way to the first-floor master bedroom, where I was packing. She stared at the trunk.

"Where are you going *this* time?" she asked.

"Canada," I said, pretending horror at the very idea. "To meet a Canuck author who wants to write a book about the French and Indian War. He's got an interesting theory that if the French had won that war, instead of the British, we'd all be eating cheese and bread and drinking red wine—and staying slim."

Taitsie picked up my African-style safari shorts. In a sour tone she asked me, "I suppose you're going to be wearing these shorts when you and your so-called *author* go on safari in the frozen Abitibi-Témiscamingue region in western Quebec?"

Taitsie had become deeply suspicious of my behavior. And no wonder. My frequent absences and the secrecy with which I conducted my life gave her reason to fear that I was seeing other *women*. And although I swore that I was faithful, my conduct caused a serious breach of trust. Our relationship had grown tense, and she wasn't shrieking *Sie müssen aufhören*! Too often these days.

Without ever discussing it, Taitsie and I had decided that having a child might somehow save our marriage, which explained how our son, Theodore J. Higginbothem IV, or Vier (German for "four"), had sprung out of the birth canal. He was the spitting image of his mother—glossy black hair, eyebrows that went straight across his forehead, and a little too much white in his eyes. The question "Are children born wild?" briefly crossed my mind, but he had grown into a fine boy. Taitsie had him working with clay when he was three years old, and by the time he was nine, he showed remarkable artistic talent. Taitsie enrolled him in Sunday art classes at the National Cathedral Elementary School.

Before long, though, Vier lost interest in art and became obsessed with sex—one more way in which he resembled his mother. Rather than spend his Sunday hour in art class working with clay, Vier wowed an audience of artsy young girls with classic comic routines that he had seen on the TV Land channel. One of his favorites was Sid Caesar's "Wings Over Boomerschnitzel."

Vier announced that he wanted to be a stand-up comedian when he grew up. When I thought deeply, which didn't happen too much, it occurred to me that his comic aspirations might be a cry for attention. My son sensed that his parents' marriage was falling apart and that he wasn't getting the love he deserved from Taitsie and me.

"Higgy," Taitsie said, "stop packing. I have something I want to say to you."

I put down the Orvis sun-reflecting hat.

"I love you, Higgy," Taitsie said. "I've loved you from the moment I first saw you across that crowded room in my father's embassy. But if you go on this trip and leave me again for one of your... *implausible* expeditions, don't expect me to be here when you come back."

"No French and Indian War?" I asked.

"No French and Indian War."

"But this book might be the long-sought cure for obesity," I said. "Imagine, a country of *slim* Americans."

"It might be the cure for obesity," she said. "But it won't be the cure for our marriage."

CHAPTER NINETEEN

As I passed through customs at Moi International Airport, I strolled alongside a skinny-legged porter who shoved my overloaded luggage cart through the crowd like a battering ram. We stopped only long enough to have my passport stamped, and playing the grand American role to the hilt, I dispensed my largesse—a few Kenyan shillings— into the palms of customs officials to make them look the other way. The port of Mombasa, the second largest city in Kenya, was one of the major routes in the world cocaine traffic. I could have been bringing in 100 kilos of nose candy, and no one would have been the wiser. I was... untouchable.

In the airport concourse, thumping Taarab music blared from loudspeakers. Hundreds of people, dressed in a riot of colorful African, Muslim, Hindu, and Western clothes, lined up behind a security railing, searching for loved ones among the faces of the disembarking passengers.

"Hey, Higgy! Over here!"

The voice calling to me was most certainly *not* that of a loved one. It belonged to Sydney Michael Green, who had been assigned to The Tchaikovsky Circle by my boss, Whitney Nutwing, without so much as a by-your-leave. Nutwing had sent Sydney Michael Green to Mombasa a week ahead of me to "prep the battlefield," as he put it.

To my disgust, I saw that a week in Africa had not done much to improve Sydney Michael Green's appearance. He had a week's worth of stubble on his double chin and twenty pounds of flesh hanging over his belt. Three inches of pants cuffs pooled around his down-a-the-heels loafers. He elbowed his way through the crowd and approached me with his arms outstretched and sweat dripping from his jowly face.

Neither Russ Slanover nor Vangie Roll understood why I had agreed to accept Sydney Michael Green as a member of our team. He and I couldn't have been more different. I was neat; he was a slob. I treated women with respect; he treated them like free samples at Macy's. I came from privilege and the best education money could buy; he was the uneducated son of a poor Irish maid and a Jewish scrap dealer.

Still, I was aware that Sydney Michael Green's skills as a field investigator were second to none among black-ops agents in the CIA. Where Vangie Roll could insinuate herself into the Chicago political and financial worlds, and Russ Slanover could hack into any computer site no matter how high and thick the Chinese Wall, Sydney Michael Green could smell trouble a hundred miles away—and deal with it quickly, effectively, and by any means necessary.

But that wasn't the real reason Whitney Nutwing had inserted Sydney Michael Green into my team. If I stumbled carrying out my assignment, Sydney Michael Green was there to assume command of The Tchaikovsky Circle. He was waiting—drooling, should I say?— in the wings to take my job.

"Here, Higgy, let me take over," Sydney Michael Green said.

He was referring to my luggage cart, not my job. I was traveling with two extra-large suitcases, three humungous duffel bags and, of course, my customary gigantic Louis Vuitton wardrobe trunk.

As we emerged from the Word War II-era airport, it was high noon, and a brutal African sun hammered on the anvil of my head. The humidity shrouded me like a blanket and I could feel the perspiration instantly seep through my natty suit. It was a hellishly long hike to the car park.

On the way we passed an attractive Hindu woman in a sari.

"Catch the red dot on that dame's forehead," Sydney Michael Green said. "I bet you thought it had something to do with her religion. No way." He smiled broadly, and I could tell he was about to launch into one of his jokes. "When one of those Hindu women gets married, she brings a dowry with her. And on her wedding night, her husband scratches off the red spot to see if he's won a convenience store, a gas station, or a donut shop."

"Syd," I said, "spare me."

I only used his nickname when he *really* got on my nerves.

"Higgy, seriously, I've got everything worked out," he said, waving his arm as though to show me the entire country. "A great driver who speaks Swahili and can also act as our interpreter. A perfect hotel. And a packed schedule of interviews over the next two days." Flecks of spit were flying through the air, and I slowed a bit to avoid the spray. "Plus, you won't believe some of the gorgeous Eastern European chicks staying at our hotel. It's like Fashion Week here in Mombasa."

Waiting for us in the car park was an NBA-sized Kenyan, who was leaning against the hood of beat-up four-door compact Peugeot. It looked like it had passed the 100,000-mile mark about 400,000 miles ago.

"Higgy, this is Abubakar," Sydney Michael Green said. "He's agreed to take care of us during our stay."

In order to look Abubakar in the eye, I had to fight off the urge to stand on my toes. Shaking hands was like putting my hand inside a warm toaster oven. How in the world did he fit inside that car?

Abubakar immediately saw that his compact Peugeot and my luggage weren't meant for each other.

"Easily solved, Mr. Sydney," he said. "A little Kenyan ingenuity."

The giant picked up my wardrobe *with one hand* and dropped it into the under-sized trunk. He covered the wardrobe with the duffels and suitcases, and tied the top, still so high it blocked the view out the back window, down with a long yellow bungee cord. I eyed the arrangement doubtfully, but I wasn't arguing with someone who could lift my steamer trunk single-handed. Sydney Michael Green and I piled into the back seat of the car, and we were off.

As our chauffeur Abubakar threaded his way through the streets of Mombasa, I glanced out the window and noticed a group of attractive women waiting at an intersection. Tall and thin, with prominent buttocks, they were dressed in brightly printed *kangas*. The traffic light changed and as the women crossed in front of our car I was mesmerized. These women didn't just walk; they seemed to undulate to the languid rhythm of some inaudible music. They reminded me of Taitsie's sculptures of nubile black women, and I wondered what Taitsie would have said—and how she might have reacted—if she had caught an eyeful of these extraordinary African women.

Sydney Michael Green opened his passenger-side door as we pulled to a stop at the entrance of the Bamburi Beach Hotel, a five-star palace that could just as easily have been in Palm Beach or La Jolla.

My top-floor suite had two bedrooms, a kitchenette, satellite TV, and an Elliptical Stair Climber tucked in the corner of the living room. I also had a view of the harbor below. Looking out, I did a double-take. There, berthed off the private dock of the Bamburi Beach Hotel, was the biggest private yacht I had ever seen in my life.

I fished out my Zeiss binoculars and focused on the ship—a battleship-sized yacht with two helipads, two swimming pools, a mini-submarine, and its own sophisticated missile-defense system. The bow was facing toward the hotel so I couldn't read the ship's name on the stern. Nor could I make out the faces of the crew who were patrolling the decks, or get a good look at the bikini-clad women sprawled on the sun deck. But in that instant, I knew that the boat could belong to only one man—my old FSB adversary and spymaster, Yurik Maligin.

CHAPTER TWENTY

The next day, with Abubakar folded up behind the wheel of our miniscule Peugeot, we drove north by northwest for several hours on the Mombasa-Nairobi highway. We spent the night in the capital city, and set out early the next morning for the remote reaches of Nyanza Province, which is on the shores of Lake Victoria. We passed no traffic to speak of, and the roads were of surprisingly high quality. Not so my mood. My gut warned me that the presence of Yurik Maligin in Kenya meant trouble.

We sped on in silence for several more hours until we approached the village of Nyang'oma Kogelo. The first thing I noticed were the huge billboards

HOME OF FAMOUS AMERICAN LEADER BARACK H. OBAMA!

VISIT HOUSE OF NEXT AMERICAN PRESIDENT!

We almost had an accident as we turned a corner and suddenly came upon a crowd of people standing in the middle of the road. Abubakar pulled the Peugeot to a stop and we got out. Sydney Michael Green went to see what all the fuss was about. The crowd was admiring a new silver convertible two-door SLR McLaren Roadster parked in front of a small, modest house. How did that get there? I wondered. I doubted they even sold McLarens in this country.

Sydney Michael Green whistled as he inspected the vehicle.

"Higgy," he said, "this little baby might be the single best automobile made today. It has an AMG V8 compressor which allows her to go over 200 miles an hour. God, I love her lines, don't you? I wonder who owns her? She costs a cool half a mil."

By now the villagers had stopped ogling the car and had turned their attention to us. There was a lot of whispering in Swahili.

"What are they saying?" I asked Abubakar.

"They are wondering if you have also come to make a gift?"

"What does that mean—a *gift*?" I asked.

Before Abubakar could inquire, the front door of the house opened and a tall, thin young man came out. He saw Sydney Michael Green and smiled.

"Ah, Mr. Green," he said in decent English, "I see that you are back. Who is your friend?"

Sydney Michael Green made the introductions.

The young man turned out to be Malik Obama, the half-brother of Barack Obama. According to my information, Malik had been the best man at Barack Obama's 1992 wedding to Michelle, and Barack Obama had been Malik's best man at *his* wedding. A native Kenyan and an accountant by training, he told me that he ran an electronics shop in Nyanbg'oma Kogelo. But when he handed me his business card, I noted that it identified him as INTERNATIONAL CONSULTANT.

"I spend several months a year in D.C.," he said by way of explanation. "Please, why don't you come in and meet my *bibi*—my grandmother?"

Malik Obama ushered us into a modest, Western-style house which would have fit into any neighborhood in the United States. A half dozen people were milling about the house.

"Cousins," explained Malik.

The house might as well have been a Barack Obama shrine. Every wall was covered with photographs of him—playing basketball in Honolulu, graduating from Columbia University, being sworn into the Illinois State Senate Chamber in Springfield. Side-by-side drawings of Barack Obama and Abraham Lincoln took up an entire wall. Obama's Harvard Law School diploma was in a frame on a small table off to the left.

Seated in a large La-Z-Boy recliner in a corner of the living room was a petite gray-haired woman. She had a shawl over her shoulders and an expression on her face that said butter wouldn't melt in her mouth.

"Gentlemen," Malik Obama said, "this is my *bibi*, Sarah Obama."

The expression on Grandma Obama's face suddenly changed, and she gave us a roguish grin. All of her teeth were capped in gold.

"*Karibu yetu!*" she said in Swahili.

Malik translated: "Welcome to our home. We love America. My grandson, Barack Hussein Obama, will one day be the president of the United States. He was sent by God to help us all."

I listened as Malik translated this extraordinary opening statement. I thought I was supposed to be in Nyang'oma Kolego, not Bethlehem. Apparently I was wrong.

"He will do great things," Grandma Obama continued. "Miracles. He is much smarter than anyone else. And with God's guidance he will make us all better."

I had a quick memory flash of Vangie Roll telling me, "*This Obama Machine is unlike anything you have ever seen.*" She might have been right. Here we were in the armpit of Africa, and we were hearing a campaign speech—not merely for the presidency of the United States, but for sainthood.

"Ma'am," I inquired, "how do you know that your grandson will become the president? He isn't even a United States Senator yet."

Malik chuckled as he heard the question, and then smiled knowingly as he spoke to Grandma Obama in Swahili. As she heard my question she, too, couldn't contain a laugh. Her gold teeth flashed as she fired back her answer.

"*Kuru*!" she said.

"Mr. Higginbothem," Malik translated, "it's *kuru*—destiny. It's predetermined. Allah has chosen her grandson... from the moment of his birth...to lead a peaceful revolution to save the world."

The mention of Obama's birth reminded me why I had come all this way. So I decided to jump right in.

"Malik, can you please ask your grandmother if it is true that her grandson was born in Mombasa?"

It seemed like Malik had been down this road before. He sighed as he began the translation, and it was clear that Grandma Obama understood what the question was even before he was finished.

Her one-word answer came back fast.

"*Ndiyo.*"

"What does *ndiyo* mean?" I asked.

"It means 'Yes' in Swahili," Malik said.

I was caught up short. This was the very answer I'd wanted.

"Malik, is your grandmother saying, 'yes,' he was born here in Kenya? Is that what she is saying?"

She answered before the translation. "*Ndiyo*," she repeated.

I suspected she understood English more than she let on.

Suddenly Malik stood up and leaned closer to his grandmother. They began a quick back-and-forth. Abubakar listened.

"He is telling her that she can't say Barack was born here in Kenya, because then he can't be president," Abubakar whispered into my ear. "But she says, she doesn't care, because Allah will make him president anyway."

After Malik had finished conferring with his grandmother, he turned back to me.

"*Bibi* says *she* was here in Kenya when my half-brother Barack was born."

The American Constitution didn't cover the whereabouts of grandmothers during the births of American citizens. But I restrained the impulse to indulge in sarcasm. Instead, I said:

"Please ask your grandmother—once again—if she was in Mombasa in the hospital when her grandson Barack Hussein Obama Jr. was born on August 4, 1961?"

Malik began the translation. But before he got out four words, Grandma Obama interrupted

"*Ndiyo*," she said. Then she added in English: "*Yes!*"

Malik seemed frustrated by her answer, and he began another heated discussion with her about American constitutional law.

"What are they saying?" I asked Abubakar.

"Malik is telling her that Mister Why asked her not to talk anymore about it," Abubakar whispered to me.

"Mister *Why*? Who's that?" I asked Abubakar.

At this point, Malik stood up and shrugged.

"Mr. Sydney," he said, "as I told you the other day, my half-brother was born in Hawaii. So there's no problem."

But there was indeed a problem. Obama's wily grandmother was adamant that he was born in Mombasa. And his half-brother Malik kept trying to switch the story.

I turned to Sydney Michael Green and signaled that I had heard enough. As we turned to leave, Grandma Obama cleared her throat. She obviously had something further to say.

"She asks if you have a gift for her," Abubakar translated.

This was the second mention of the subject of gifts. I had been slow on the pickup before, but now I smiled. I reached into my pocket for a few Kenyan shillings. You could be cheap in this country, and people would shower you with thanks.

Yet, Grandma Obama gave me a look like "Are you kidding?" She reached into her purse and fished around, finally coming up with a business card.

She said—and again Abubakar translated—"We have a friend who gave us the gift of a new car. Perhaps you will give us a boat?"

She handed the card to Sydney Michael Green, who glanced at it and gave it to me. It read, YURIK MALIGIN, MONTE CARLO.

Mister Why was Yurik Maligin.

I felt the blood drain from my face.

CHAPTER TWENTY-ONE

When Sydney Michael Green and I arrived back at the Bamburi Beach Hotel in Mombasa an envelope was waiting for me at the front desk.

Yurik Maligin Requests
The Pleasure of Comrade Higgy's Company
For Drinks and Other Assorted Pleasures
At 8:30 O'clock Aboard *The Escape*

RSVP the Front Desk of the Bamburi

The invitation confirmed my worst fear—namely, that Yurik Maligin was on the same trail as I was. But why would the Russian master spy be interested in an obscure Illinois politician who was running for the United States Senate? That didn't make any sense. Unless Whitney Nutwing was right and Barack Obama was already running for president in 2008.

On the other hand, I wasn't going to pass up a party on a mega yacht. Free drinks, pretty girls, sumptuous dinner—of course, the only reason I was going was to engage in surreptitious activities. I'd let everyone else get loaded, then take a leisurely stroll to see what I would see.

The hotel launch took us out to *The Escape*. I was dressed in my Humphrey Bogart white dinner jacket, looking ultra debonair. Sydney Michael Green, on the other hand, was channeling Johnny Depp: the unshaven look; an open-collared, untucked yellow shirt; no jacket; no socks; casual loafers.

Maligin's maitre d', a tall, leggy blonde named Yelena, greeted us on board. She spoke English with a slight French accent. Her white mini-skirt was little more than a maxi belt. She was wearing a pair of Stuart Weitzman "Diamond Dream" shoes, which, as an aficionado of fashion, I knew the price tag: a cool $500,000.

Yelena took us on a tour of *The Escape*: the swimming pools, the helipads, and the bridge, which featured an anti-paparazzi "shield" that fired a laser beam at a camera, destroying all digital photographs. I carefully memorized all the places I might want to visit later.

"The General," she explained, referring to Maligin by his old KGB rank, "wants to prevent pirates. So we have missile-proof windows on every window."

Next, we took an elevator to a lower deck. As we got off, I thought I heard the sound of dogs barking.

"Do you keep a dog kennel on board?" I asked Yelena.

I pictured Maligin using a brace of bloodthirsty Dobermans during one of his torture sessions.

"You'll have to ask the General about that," Yelena said.

"Have to ask me about *what*?"

Yurik Maligin, all five feet of him, approached with a huge grin and an extended hand. He exuded warmth and bonhomie. And he already reeked of Scotch, his favorite libation.

"And this must be the infamous Sydney Michael Green that our Federal Security Service so hopes will replace Comrade Higgy. Welcome aboard, Comrade Sydney! Welcome aboard, Comrade Higgy!"

He led us into a small lounge, where an Asian waitress, dressed in a short, white mini-skirt like Yelena's, asked us for our drink orders.

"Higgy," Maligin said, "I have broken out a case of your old favorite, Hidalgo Manzanilla Pastrana sherry. And Comrade Sydney drinks Bailie Nicol Jarvie, a wonderful blended whisky. My research tells me you will drink just about anything, but that Bailie is your favorite, no?"

Sydney Michael Green glanced at me. I knew what that look meant. The enemy was already treating him like my equal.

"Yurik," I said, "I'm off the sauce. I'll just have a soft drink or iced tea."

Maligin seemed offended by my teetotalarism. "I heard about you and Taitsie," he said. "My condolences."

"Let's not discuss our private lives tonight." Or any night, I added to myself.

Maligin led us over to a sofa and two chairs, and opened a small humidor. Inside were two-dozen Saint Luis Rey Lonsdale CAB 50 cigars.

"Smoke?"

Sydney Michael Green and I both happily accepted, and Maligin clipped our cigars and chose one for himself.

Just then a disheveled man, possibly inebriated, stumbled into the lounge. He looked familiar, but at first I couldn't place him. Then I remembered. We had met in London during the Bill Clinton Matter. This was Charnofsky, the assistant Maligin had ordered to pick up dog poop with his bare hands.

Maligin's face turned red and his body tensed. He snapped at Charnofsky—two quick words in Russian—and the man was gone.

"Sorry," he said, "that fucking Charnofsky is causing me big trouble these days. Big trouble…"

Maligin looked away for a moment, and then his face rearranged itself into a more placid expression. Music and a deep bass beat came from down the hall. But Maligin ignored it as he drew on his Lonsdale and exhaled.

"So, Higgy," he finally said, "what brings you this far from home?"

"I could ask you the same thing," I said. "I don't picture you cruising the east coast of Africa too often."

He hesitated—a dramatic pause—then whispered, "You'd be surprised the places I sometime appear."

The Asian waitress returned, and served us our drinks along with platters of steamed vegetables. She placed small napkins and cocktail forks in front of each of us, and then left.

I was about to probe Maligin again, when the door burst open and two tall, vivacious young women almost fell into the room. A redhead and a brunette, they were wearing short shorts and halter tops and spike heels. Both were laughing and seemed to be high on something. Their arms were wrapped around each as they fell onto a sofa across from us, with the brunette rolling on top of the redhead. I barely glanced at them, but they were going at it like porn stars.

"Higgy...Sydney...perhaps you would like to watch while we chat?" Maligin said.

Maligin's girls were all "Sparrows"—FSB-trained enticers who were expert at getting men to talk. I ignored them, not stealing even the slightest peek.

"Yurik," I said, "whenever we show up in the same city, it usually means we're on the same trail, doesn't it?"

"Higgy," he replied, also ignoring the women, "I have such fond memories of London. What trouble we caused each other!"

The door opened again, and this time Charnofsky came in looking furious. His hair was mussed, and he weaved as he walked toward Maligin, who saw him coming and stood up.

"You drunken pig!" Maligin shouted. "How dare you defy me?"

Charnofsky lunged toward Maligin who, despite his small stature, was surprisingly strong and agile. In less than a second he had flipped Charnofsky onto the floor, seized his right hand and placed it on the table, grabbed a cocktail fork, and stabbed it into the back of his hand.

Charnofsky screamed.

Maligin laughed. “You stupid fucker!” he shouted. “The next time you try that it will be Sebastopol for you!”

Still smoking our cigars, Maligin and I stood up and said good-bye to Sydney Michael Green, who had by this time joined the two panting girls on the sofa. I had my reasons for not warning Sydney Michael Green about the intentions of these “Sparrows”; depending on what information the girls tried to pry out of him, I could determine how far Maligin had progressed in *his* investigation. I could also happily report to Nutwing that Syd had not a smidgen of self-control when it came to women.

“Higgy, you are staring with such longing at them. Are you sure you don—?”

“Would I? Are you asking, would I? No, of course not.”

Maligin and I emerged onto one of the open decks. It was a beautiful, warm night. The stars were out. The Bamburi Beach Hotel was lit up off to the ship’s port side.

Leaning over the railing, I turned toward my longtime adversary. “I have a question for you, Yurik. How can you work for a thug like Vladimir Putin. He’s no better than a gangster.”

Maligin took a long draw on his cigar and then flipped the stub into the water far below. “Higgy,” he said, “you Americans are hypocrites. In one breath, you lecture us Russians about freedom and democracy. And then in the next, your CIA creates a secret directorate, headed by you, with the expressed goal of placing your hand-picked man in the White House."

He placed a hand on my shoulder. "Let's not argue," he said. "Are you sure I can't offer you some entertainment down below?"

"No thank you," I said.

"You need to get over Taitsie," he said. "Higgy, I have every type of woman down below. Perhaps one or two of them could make you forget...."

But nothing could make me forget Taitsie. I threw my cigar over the railing, too.

"I should be going," I said. "Let's find Sydney Michael Green, and we'll be off."

A few minutes later, a surprisingly alert Sydney Michael Green appeared and we boarded the launch back to the Bamburi Hotel.

"Tell me something," I said after we were well out of electronic earshot of the yacht. "Down below decks....did those girls ask you any questions?"

He grinned. "Yeah. They asked me what I wanted them to do to me!"

"I don't mean *that*," I said. "Did either one of them ask you what we were doing here in Mombasa?"

He shook his head. "Nope"

"*Damn!*" I said.

"What's the matter?"

"They didn't try to get information out of you, which can only mean one thing," I said. "*They* know things about Barack Obama that *we* don't know."

I recalled Vangie Roll telling me about the strange look that came over Barack Obama's face back at that gym in Chicago when she asked him about the circumstances surrounding his birth. My spirits sank as I wondered whether, in exchange for that half-a-million-dollar McLaren Roadster, Grandma "Bibi" Obama had given Yurik Maligin documents proving where Obama had been born. If so, did those documents demonstrate beyond a shred of doubt that Obama had been born in Mombasa and that he was a Muslim instead of what he claimed to be—a Christian? And where did that leave Obama's claim that *he* had incontrovertible proof that he was born on *American* soil—in Hawaii?

More to the point, where did all this leave The Tchaikovsky Circle and me? I turned to Sydney Michael Green.

"Tell Abubakar to pack my Louis Vuitton steamer trunk," I said. "We're out of here."

"Already?" he said, disappointment written all over his face. "Geez, Higgy, I was just beginning to meet some nice girls."

"Get on the horn and requisition one of The Tchaikovsky Circle's Gulfstreams," I said. "You and I have a twenty-one-hour flight ahead of us. We're going to Honolulu."

CHAPTER TWENTY-TWO

From the airport in Honolulu, Sydney Michael Green and I took a taxi directly to Kapi'olani Medical Center, one of *two* Hawaiian hospitals that claimed to be the site of Barack Obama's 1961 birth. This guy's popularity was unbelievable. Even as a baby, everybody wanted a piece of him.

Waiting for us there was our red-bearded colleague Russ Slanover, The Tchaikovsky Circle's brilliant computer hacker. Russ embraced me warmly, then looked over my shoulder at Sydney Michael Green.

"Hello…*Grrr-eeen*," he said.

"Hello…*Whiz* Bang," Sydney Michael Green replied.

These two did not get along. Sydney Michael Green felt intellectually inferior to Russ Slanover. And Russ suspected that Sydney Michael Green was angling to replace me as head of The Tchaikovsky Circle. That meant Russ would have to explain his brilliance to a moron.

Both of them were right.

We walked into a scene of bedlam on the hospital grounds. A line of several hundred boisterous people—most of them middle-aged and white and wearing funny hats—was filing into a Barnum & Bailey-sized tent. A huge banner, fluttering from the top of the center pole, displayed the logo of the Fox News Channel and the face of Sean Hannity.

"What's going on, Russ?" I asked.

"Sean Hannity flew in earlier today to do a live broadcast about a newly formed organization called Only The Truth," Russ explained. "His guest is the head of the group—a female Polish-American Marine Corps sergeant with a huge following here in Hawaii."

I shrugged. "Anything with Hannity is all right with me."

We went inside and took our seats. Up on the raised stage, under the blinding TV lights, Sean Hannity sat facing his guest.

"Welcome to a special edition of *Hannity*," he said. "Today, we're going to focus on a new conservative movement called Only The Truth. Please give a warm welcome to its leader...Dagmar D. Dagmar!"

The audience erupted in applause, whistles, hoots, hollers and assorted victory cries.

"Welcome, Dagmar, if I may call you that," Hannity said.

"You can call me Dagmar or you can call me Dagmar, just as you please," Dagmar D. Dagmar said, sitting ramrod stiff in her chair and staring Hannity right in the eye.

"Well, let's get started," Hannity said. "Tell us in your own words about your organization, Only The Truth."

"To begin with, we've assembled convincing evidence—*proof* really—that the United States government was behind the 9/11 attack," Dagmar D. Dagmar said. "It was an inside job all the way. We also have proof that the Apollo Program was all faked. Man never walked on the Moon. It was all faked in a secret underground TV studio at the Jet Propulsion Laboratory in Pasadena. And we also have evidence that John F. Kennedy is still alive. Most of his brain was blown away in Dallas and he's a vegetable living in a secret wing of Parkland Memorial Hospital. Before she died, Judith Campbell Exner used to visit him and bring him his favorite New England clam chowder."

Hannity was smiling away. "Could he eat the soup?" he asked.

"He couldn't digest the pieces of clams," she replied sadly. "They got stuck in his colostomy bag."

"Dagmar, you're a great American," Hannity said, swiveling his chair and facing the packed auditorium. "We'll get into more detail about Only the Truth with Dagmar D. Dagmar after a brief commercial break. That's straight ahead. And don't forget, you in the TV audience can vote on who gets the Freedom Edition Jeep Grand Cherokee and a trip for two to the Freedom Concert. Our Hannity video contest finalists are on Hannity dot com. Be right back."

The TV lights snapped off and the stage went dark. Hannity consulted the script on his lap. A makeup woman came over and powdered his nose and forehead and applied some shoe black to his sideburns. After a while, a producer appeared behind one of the cameras and began the countdown…four… three…two…one…

"And we're *back* with my *guest*, Sergeant Dagmar D. Dagmar."

"Sergeant *major*," Dagmar D. Dagmar said, correcting Hannity. She tapped the stripes on her sleeve. "I'll never get a promotion to warrant officer because of my involvement with our organization, Only The Truth. The Marine Corps can't *handle* the truth."

"Well, Sergeant Major," Hannity said, "I'm sure you're aware that some people—some simpering, puerile, blockheaded liberals—would challenge the veracity of what you've told me."

"Not Oliver Stone," Dagmar D. Dagmar said. "And he's a liberal."

"That's true, but what about *Sharon* Stone?" Hannity asked.

"What does Sharon Stone have to do with it?"

"She's Oliver Stone's wife, isn't she?" Hannity said.

"No she's not."

"Are you sure?" Hannity said. "They have the same last name."

"A lot of celebrities have the last name of Stone."

"Name one," Hannity said. "I *challenge* you."

Dagmar D. Dagmar thought for a long time, then finally said: "I can't."

"You see," Hannity said, smiling triumphantly into the camera. "Anyway, now I want to talk about someone with another strange last name—a rising star from the state of Illinois…a Democratic candidate for the United States Senate…

a far-left Marxist politician by the name of Barack Hussein Obama. There's talk that he may run for president in four years. Have you ever heard of this guy?"

"Have I *heard* of Barack Obama!" said Dagmar D. Dagmar, slapping her muscular thigh and breaking out in a derisive laugh. "Are you *kidding*? "Was Alger Hiss a Soviet spy? Did Joseph McCarthy have a piece of paper containing a list of Commies? Does fluoride rot your teeth? Of course I've *heard* of Barack Obama."

"Good," Hannity said, "then let's focus on the question of Barack Obama's birth. Was he—as he and his campaign claim—born here in Honolulu on April 4, 1961, which would make him eligible to run for the highest office in the land? Or has he conspired to hide the fact that he was born somewhere else?"

"Our organization, Only the Truth, has assembled convincing evidence—*proof* really—that Obama was *not* born in Hawaii," Dagmar D. Dagmar said. "It's all a gigantic conspiracy by leftists to plant a Muslim in the Oval Office and to teach our children to wear shoes with Velcro instead of laces so they can take off their shoes when they come home."

"You say *proof*," Hannity said. "What *proof* do you have that Senator Obama was not born here?"

Dagmar D. Dagmar produced a document and held it up in front of the TV camera.

"This is a Hawaiian birth certificate," she said. "Obama says this certificate proves he was born in Hawaii. But, Sean, take a closer look. You'll see that there's no state seal on it!"

"Wow," Hannity said. "You *are* a great American, Dagmar!"

The members of the audience went wild. They began chanting: "Only the truth…only the truth…only the truth…"

"Okay, okay," Hannity said, holding up a hand to quiet down the audience. "Wait a second. Also with us today are two obstetricians – both of whom claim to have birthed Barack Obama here in Honolulu! Help me welcome the first one—Dr. Benny Agbayani, the chief of obstetrics here at Kapi'olani Medical Center."

Doctor Agbayani, a short, plump, dark-skinned man, walked onto the stage. He squinted into the TV lights, held up a palm to shield his eyes and then settled into a seat next to Dagmar D. Dagmar.

"Doctor," Hannity said, "is it true that when you were a young resident, you participated in the birth of Barack Obama?"

"Oh yes," Agbayani said, "I remember that birth very well. It was a magical experience. He was such a lovely baby."

"But, doctor, there are no hospital records of that birth," Hannity said. "So how can you be certain that you performed this birth more than forty years ago?"

Dr. Agbayani opened a box and removed a specimen jar. He held it up toward the TV camera.

"I knew then that the baby was going to be special," he said, "so I preserved his umbilical cord and his cord blood. And here it *is*!"

The crowd was stunned into stone, cold silence.

"Now," said Hannity, "let me introduce the *second* doctor—Dr. Dr. Louis Gabaldoni from Queen's Medical Center here in Honolulu."

Gabaldoni, a tall, thin man with a shock of white hair, appeared from the other wing of the stage. He appeared to be in an agitated state. Even before he reached his seat, he began talking in a very loud voice.

"This is ridiculous!" he said. "Ree-*dick*-you-louse! Barack Obama was born in *our* hospital and I have the preserved placenta to prove it!"

He held up a jar with a reddish gooey object in it.

"Well, there you have it, folks— *two* doctors from *two* different hospitals who *both* claim to have birthed Barack Obama," Hannity said. He turned to Dagmar D. Dagmar. "Now, do you know what I call *that*?"

"No, what?" she asked.

"I call *that* fair and balanced," said Hannity.

CHAPTER TWENTY-THREE

Dr. Agbayani's umbilical cord blood and Dr. Galdoni's placenta were shipped from Hawaii to CIA and FBI laboratories on the mainland to be analyzed. Only the most senior government employees with the highest security clearance were assigned to the project. Since these people were guaranteed a month's vacation plus compensatory time off for overtime and ten days of sick leave, they were at their desks an average of less than ten hours a week. From this truncated workweek, the government workers subtracted an hour and twenty minutes each day for lunch plus morning and afternoon coffee breaks. As a result, they made very slow progress and the search for Barack Obama's identity dragged on and on.

On November 6, 2004—the Saturday after Barack Obama was elected to the United States Senate—Vangie Roll and I met in a Southside Chicago diner for breakfast. She was wearing a ruffled purple dress with a plunging neckline, and I was trying not to stare down it all the way to her navel. I could get pretty close, most of the way over the stomach....

A frowzy old waitress in a dirty white uniform came over to our table and stood there chewing gum with sharp cracking sounds.

"Whadda ya have?" she asked in a peevish tone of voice.

"The waffles with well-done bacon and a cup of black coffee," I said.

"I'll have what *he's* having," Vangie said.

"Hey, ain't that a line from *When Harry Met Sally*?" the waitress said.

"Yes, and we're just *like* Harry and Sally," Vangie said. "The sex part always gets in our way."

After the waitress had left, I said: "Why did you have to say that?"

"Because even though you like to deny it, you really want to nail me," Vangie said, leaning forward.

Finally, I thought I saw her navel, just a precious glimpse. "No I don't," I said.

"Yes you do."

"Don't."

"Do."

"All right," I said. "*Enough.* Let's get down to business."

"Well, as you know," Vangie began, sitting back in her seat, "my Mom's still a member in good standing of the Illinois Bar, and a few weeks ago she was appointed by Mayor Richard Daley to serve on the board of the Chicago Low Income Trust—CLIT for short.

"As the mayor's representative in our community, Mom's supposed to recommend people and businesses to receive tax-exempt grants. There's a lot of money behind CLIT, and as you might imagine, Mom's been inundated with requests from a bunch of gonifs. The chief gonif is a local minister, the Reverend Jeremiah Wright, who invited us to his church.

"Next to pulling your leg, Higgy, there's nothing Mom loves more than going to church, so off we went for Sunday services. When we arrived at the church, you'd think the British royal family had shown up. Three huge men were at the curb to help Mom into her wheelchair, and a group from the ladies auxiliary rushed up to me with a corsage of white lilies.

"Waiting for us at the vestry door was the Reverend Wright himself, a light-skinned African-American man, wearing a *kufu*, a traditional African cap, and a dark blue dashiki with gold embroidered neck and sleeves. And I'm talking about embroidery made of *real* gold thread.

"I had on in my regular Sunday-go-to-church outfit, including a pair of Capezio flats so I wouldn't tower over the men. The Reverend Wright's in his sixties and on the short side, but that didn't stop him from giving me the once-over from my head to my Capezios.

"Then he said, 'I hope you two will come back later tonight to attend a campaign meeting for our brother, Barack Obama.' "

"Wait a second," I said. "Why would there be a campaign meeting four days *after* Obama won election to the United States Senate?"

"I'll tell you why," Vangie said, warming up to her delicious news. "The Reverend Wright says this is going to be the *first* meeting of Barack Obama's 2008 *presidential* campaign."

Neon lights started flashing in my head. The game was on. "Vangie," I said, "you've got to get me into that meeting."

CHAPTER TWENTY-FOUR

That night, when Vangie Roll and I arrived at Trinity United Church of Christ, the building was lit up like a Christmas tree. People were scrambling all over the place. Vangie introduced me to the Reverend Jeremiah Wright using the alias we had worked out—Alfred Douglas, the treasurer of CLIT.

"Good to meet you, Alfie," the Reverend said. "Vangie tells me you're the guy who has his finger on CLIT."

"That's right."

"Well, Alfie, it's always a pleasure to meet the man who can pull the trigger." He laughed uproariously.

Boy, what a sense of humor. I could tell we were in for a long night.

He took us in a private elevator down to his office. The entire basement level was a high-tech command post for the Reverend Wright's organization. Phones were ringing. Fax machines were spitting out documents. It was like the corporate HQ of a Fortune 500 company—and yet all this activity was taking place in a church basement on a Saturday evening at 6 P.M.

"This is really impressive," Vangie said.

"Vangie, there's much more going on in black churches these days than just gospel music," the Reverend Wright informed us. "Those white born-again churches—mega-churches, they call them—those churches have expanded their reach through the use of TV. They've got tens of thousands of congregants, and each one of them pays through the nose. That young preacher with the hot wife, Joel Osteen—the Bushes pray there when they're in Houston—Osteen grosses over $50 million a year. And all his books are on the best-seller lists. He even has his own jet. But we in the African community haven't caught up with the Osteens of this world. Not yet, anyway. I aim to make Trinity United Church the flagship of a national African church for all our brothers and sisters. And Barack Obama's going to be the poster boy for my church."

All the time he was talking, he kept staring at my solid-gold Patek Philippe watch. If he wasn't a holy man, I'd swear he wanted to rip it right off my wrist.

We entered the Reverend Wright's conference room. It reminded me of the White House Situation Room—a sleek, long table with high-backed leather chairs and drop-down screens for video conference calls. The Reverend Wright pointed to a wall of signed photographs and memorabilia. The biggest picture showed President Lyndon Baines Johnson laying in a hospital bed in pajamas next to a much younger-looking Jeremiah Wright in medical scrubs. It was autographed: "To Jeremiah, thank you for getting me through tough times. I owe you my life. Sincerely, Lyndon."

"I was the president's navy nurse in Bethesda when he had gall bladder surgery," Wright announced proudly. "Lyndon Johnson and I established a deep bond and stayed in touch for the rest of the president's life. That man taught me everything I know about politics, including how to spend money you ain't got." He gave my watch another significant look. The next thing I knew, he'd be asking for it as a "donation."

He moved down the wall to the next group of photographs. Most were of hairy, disheveled white guys— beards, mustaches, fu manchus—in ratty-looking jackets, baggy shirts, and blue jeans.

One autograph read, "To J. Wright, a true Revolutionary! Love, Jerry."

The next one read, "Jeremiah, the Establishment will one day learn you are the Wright man to change our corrupt society. Best Wishes, Tom."

And yet another read, "In order to bring about radical reform of this goddamn America, you have to be radical, man! I am with you always!" It was signed, "Abbie.

"These white boys might as well be brothers," the Reverend Wright sighed. "They went to jail for us. True heroes—they took it to the streets right here in Chicago. Jerry Rubin, Tom Hayden, and Abbie Hoffman. Dear, dear friends of mine. I was so sad when Abbie passed. We held a service here for him. Imagine that! A Jew boy honored in this African church!"

I looked over to see how Vangie was taking this, and she rolled her eyes.

"Now," the Reverend said, "let me show you my real dream."

He led us over to a low table. On it stood an architectural model of a McMansion complete with a turret, a glass-enclosed arboretum, an indoor pool, and a basketball court. With a finger he pressed down one of the hoops, and when he let it go, it sprang right back up.

"My fantasy home," he said. "And thanks to our Sunday collections, my generous congregants are making my fantasy come true. I'm movin' into this house in a few months."

Then he pointed across the room to a life-size color photograph of himself with another smiling, happy-looking man. Underneath this photograph, on Illinois State Senate stationery, was a letter addressed to the Reverend with these words:

"To my real African father. Thank you for giving me the audacity of hope. Sincerely Yours, Barack."

People started filing into the conference room. The Reverend Wright took his place at the head of the table, and the others arranged themselves in pre-assigned seats.

"Good evening, brothers and sisters," the Reverend Wright said. "Most of you are already acquainted with the attractive lady in the elegant dress who's sitting at the other end of the table from me. For those of you who haven't had the pleasure, let me introduce Valerie Jarrett."

Valerie Jarrett was dressed in an elegant red suit with a matching camisole, and big pearl earrings. She nodded to the people around the table.

"Valerie's worked for the late Mayor Harold Washington and the Daley family," the Reverend Wright continued. "She knows where all the bodies are buried. She gave Michelle Obama her first major job, and helped run Barack's Senate campaign. If you want Barack to do something, there are only two people he's not going to say no to: Valerie Jarrett and Michelle Obama. Valerie understands Barack. She 'gets' him. She's his intermediary to the outside world. We're proud to have Valerie here with us tonight."

There was a polite round of applause.

"Now," he continued, "the white guy sitting on Valerie's right..."

The people at the table began to titter, and I looked hard at the semi-old geezer Wright was pointing at. He looked familiar, but I couldn't place him.

"...the white fellow is Professor Bill Ayres. He's known for a lot of things, including founding the Weather Underground, a Communist revolutionary group that bombed the Pentagon and the United States Capitol during the Vietnam War. He happened to kill a couple of people along the way, but that's neither here nor there. He's a reputable citizen nowadays, a professor in the College of Education at the University of Illinois, and an adviser on education to Mayor Daley."

Reputable or not, I could still use him to tar Obama.

"Sitting to Bill's right is his wife, Bernardine Dohrn. If you think Bill Ayres was a hothead, then you haven't Googled Bernardine. Back in the good old days, she made some choice comments about the murders by the Charles Manson gang of pregnant actress Sharon Tate and her rich friends. As I recall, Bernardine said, 'Dig it! First they killed those pigs and then they put a fork in pig Tate's belly. Wild! Offing those rich pigs with their own forks and knives, and then eating a meal in the same room, far out! The Weathermen dig Charles Manson!'"

The Reverend Wright was a regular goldmine. Or should I say arsenal, because he was handing me weapons that I would employ without a shred of mercy.

"Brothers and sisters," the Reverend Wright continued, "last Tuesday's victory was just step one of our master plan. And it was the easiest step. There can be no rest. The next step begins tomorrow morning in D.C. We are going to make Barack Obama president of the United States in 2008. And that's why we're here tonight.

"Right on, bro," someone shouted.

"You tell it the way it is, Rev."

"You each have a copy of the campaign plan in front of you," Wright continued. "Please let's go to section one."

Everyone opened the thick, three-ring binder.

"First," the Reverend Wright said, "we have to introduce our candidate for 2008 to America. And do it in a way that doesn't make them afraid."

He pressed a button on the console in front of him. An image appeared on the overhead video screen.

"Honest Abe Lincoln. From Illinois. Tall. Thin. A lawyer. Almost no prior elected experience. A great orator."

The Reverend looked around the table, and then resumed.

"We are going to convince America that this man Obama is the reincarnation of Abe Lincoln. And if we say it enough, they'll believe it."

Heads nodded around the table.

"Now, let's address the key issue: money. With it, we can go all the way. Without it, we will be chasing our tails for four years." He glanced my way, and I instinctively placed my hand over my watch.

A young black man with a shaved head raised his hand and waited to be called on.

"Yes, Van," the Reverend said. "People, this is Van Jones. He's the guy who pointed out—correctly, I might add—that the Bush administration *allowed* the September 11 attacks to occur as a pretext for war in the Middle East. Van's got something to report to us."

"I'm just back from overseas," Van Jones said. "I've been assured that we have large sources of funding from China, Russia, and Indonesia. In addition, Iran and the Arab Emirates are eager to come onboard the campaign."

"Really?" the Reverend asked. "I thought foreigners were prohibited by law from donating to American political campaigns."

"Well, Reverend," Van Jones said, "I spoke to an aide to George Soros about that and ..."

The Reverend Wright interrupted: "If Mr. Soros' aide says it's okay, then that's good enough for me. Let's move on."

He pressed another button on his console and the words MEDIA RELATIONS appeared on the overhead video screens.

"Where are we on this?" Wright asked.

David Axelrod, who was Obama's chief political strategist, stood up.

"We have loyalists in just about every newsroom in the country," he said. "We have firm commitments from the editors at the *New York Times* and the *Washington Post* that they are on Barack's team. CNN and MSNBC are like dogs in heat calling me every day asking, 'When is Barack going to announce? We want to help.' Katie Couric is all over me urging Barack to run—even though she says in public that she still loves Hillary! But Katie's for Barack all the way. In fact, she told me that she'd like to go out on a date with Barack—if he were only younger."

A mischievous look came over the Reverend Wright's face. He pointed across the table at Vangie Roll.

"This attractive *single* woman is Vangie Roll, a lawyer in our neighborhood," he said. "Her mom's a member of CLIT—the Chicago Low Income Trust. And Vangie's a friend of Trinity United. Vangie, let me ask you a question. When a new gentleman suitor comes chasing after you, under which scenario does he get more heated up: when you hint you might be receptive to his advances, or when you slam the door in his face and say, 'No way. I'm not interested. Period'?"

"I'm really the wrong person to ask," Vangie said, stealing a glance at me. "When it comes to one particular man, I don't know how to play hard to get."

"But you get my point!" the Reverend said. "We have Barack play hard to get for the next few months. Slam the door on running for president in 2008. And the result will be everyone will want him *even more!*"

"That's very interesting," Vangie said, looking at me straight in the face. "Maybe it's time for me to change *my* game plan, too."

CHAPTER TWENTY-FIVE

When the meeting finally broke up, the Reverend Wright slipped Vangie Roll a note asking her to stay behind. He waited until all the others had left the room, and then went over to where Vangie was sitting next to me. He placed his hands gently on her shoulders, and began giving her what could only be described as an erotic back rub. He seemed pretty old to be sexing up a girl like that, but what did I know?

"How 'bout you and me, we go for a drink at Bee's?" he said in a singsong, seductive rhyme.

Vangie looked over at me.

"Hell," the Reverend said, removing his hands from Vangie's back, "if it'd make you feel more comfortable, we can take Alfie along with us. Show him how brothers and sistas lax out at a jazz joint."

I suddenly was feeling very possessive, although I don't know why. "Sounds good to me," I said.

"Okay," Vangie said, "let's do it."

The Reverend shed his dashiki and replaced it with a navy blue merino ribbed cashmere turtleneck sweater. Over this, he hung a thick gold chain necklace that matched his oversized gold pinkie ring.

"Follow me," he said, leading us through a side door.

Outside, waiting for us at the curb, was the largest limousine I had ever seen in my life. It was long and black and squarish, and looked more like a railroad freight car than a limousine.

"This beauty's called the Ghost Rider," the Reverend Wright said with undisguised pride. "She's got a 1,800-watt Sony surround-sound system, a large-screen TV, a full bar, a bathroom, and even a queen-sized bed." He chuckled lewdly. "That bed's seen lots of action, Jackson."

"Impressive," Vangie said, not sounding the least bit tempted.

"When you get in and take a ride, you'll think you've gone to heaven and died," the Reverend said, reverting to rhyme.

He looked up and down the street. "But first, we gotta find my wife," he added impatiently.

A chauffeur in full livery—gray cap with matching gray suit and gloves —hopped out of the limousine.

"Good evenin', Rev."

"Malcolm," Wright said, "where the hell's Randa?"

"Don't know, Rev," Malcolm replied. "Told her what time you said to be here. Told her to be on time *this* time."

"Did you try her on her cell phone?"

"Yes, Rev, but you know the missus—she never answers that tiny little phone. Even after you changed the ring to Jelly Roll's 'Black Bottom Stomp.' "

"Well, we're goin' to Bee's," Wright told Malcolm. "But first, we gonna drop off Mrs. Wright at the house." He looked at his watch. "If we can *find* her. Where's that woman *at*?"

Just then an attractive African-American woman in a J. Mendel cinnamon-colored sheared mink coat and carrying a red Hermès Kelly bag came stumbling toward us on four-inch spike heels. She was juggling several large shopping bags—from Gucci, Dolce & Gabbana, Etro, and Jimmy Choo.

"Here I am...here I am..." she said, out of breath. "Sorry I'm late."

Malcolm the chauffeur rushed forward and relieved her of the shopping bags.

"I was at the Sackler Gallery with my women's museum group," she said. "There was a wonderful exhibit of early prints by Whistler."

"Folks," the Reverend said, "this is my aesthetically pleasing, exorbitantly dressed, artistically bent wife, Randa Reed Wright.

We shook hands.

"Randa, this here is Alfie Douglas from CLIT, and this here is Vangie Roll, the new church member I been tellin' you 'bout."

Randa Wright gave Vangie a long, withering look of female mistrust. Then she climbed into the backseat. Vangie sat in the middle and the Reverend on the other side. I sat on one of the jump seats.

As soon as Malcolm maneuvered the huge vehicle into a traffic lane, Vangie made a stab at breaking the ice.

"Tell me," she said to Randa Reed Wright, "how did you and your husband meet?"

"Like one of those Sabine women," Randa replied.

"Pardon me," Vangie said.

"You ever see that painting by Peter Paul Rubens in the National Gallery in London?" Randa said. "*The Rape of the Sabines*, it's called. Well, I was a Sabine woman. My first husband, Mister Reed, and I went to Jeremiah at Trinity United for marriage counseling. And instead of being a trustworthy counselor, Jeremiah was hinky. He just snatched me away from Mister Reed. Just like one of those Sabine women!"

"And you loved every minute of it," the Reverend said. "L-U-V-E-D!"

Randa didn't bother to answer him, and another period of strained silence descended upon our little group in the limousine. Then, all at once, Randa Reed Wright let out an ear-splitting scream. Someone flipped on the overhead light, and I watched as Randa reached down and picked up a small, limp object between her thumb and forefinger.

"What the…" she said.

She was holding a pair of red-fringed, black-laced panties. She read the label out loud. "Guia La Bruna. These go for seven hundred fifty dollars, and they ain't mine, I can tell you that!"

She turned toward Vangie.

"And they ain't yours either," she said. "They're too small for your ass."

Then she turned on her husband. "Who you Sabine-ing now?"

I was watching with rapt attention. This was better than reality television. To my amazement, the Reverend Wright didn't miss a beat.

"Randa, baby," he said, "I don't know what y'all talkin' about. I have no idea where these panties came from. Maybe Malcolm brought a girl back here and did the nasty when I wasn't lookin'. Maybe… *whatever.* All I know is I had nothing whatsoever to do with these panties. So help me God."

"Jeremiah, why do I not believe a word you're saying?" Randa said, shaking her head. "Why do I think your thick fingers were all over these panties when they were on that anorexic little bitch, Nailah Fonseca? You nailin' Nailah? Is that what this is"—she shoved the panties into the Reverend Wright's face and rubbed them in—"is that what this is all about?"

"Now, Randa, be reasonable," the Reverend said. "Nailah Fonseca is havin' a difficult time, what with her husband gettin' two consecutive life sentences and all. She came to me for counseling."

Just then the limousine drew to a stop and Malcolm opened Randa's door, effectively putting an end to the marital donnybrook. But as Randa got out of the car, she gave her husband a final steely look.

"One drink down at Bee's with these folks," she said, "and then you come straight home, you hear?"

CHAPTER TWENTY-SIX

Less than a half hour later, we arrived in a dark, deserted area of South Chicago warehouses, a few blocks east of the Dan Ryan Expressway. You could see the illuminated outline of the Chicago Skyway toll bridge against the night sky. In front of the jazz club, a long line of people, both black and white, was waiting to get in—men in fur coats and fedoras, women in tight-fitting, brightly colored dresses, some of them trimmed with velvet fringes.

"Hey, Jeremiah," a voice called out, "come on up here to the head of the line."

"Hey, Duke," the Reverend called back.

He motioned for us to follow him. At the door, the Reverend and Duke exchanged a soul brother handshake.

"Duke's been the doorman at Queen Bee's forever," the Reverend told us. "Bee's the last of the old Chicago jazz clubs. How's it hanging, Duke?"

"Life's sweet, Jeremiah. Except, we don't call it Queen Bee's no mo'. It's Lee's Unleaded Blues now."

"Whatever," the Reverend said.

He tipped Duke, and led Vangie and me behind the velvet rope and inside the club. It was a small, oddly shaped room, dark and thick with smoke. I smelled more pot than Pall Malls. There were mirrors and deep red carpeting everywhere. The painted walls were covered with old black and white headshots of great blues musicians, and framed 45 and 33 rpm vinyl records.

As we made our way along a red-leather bar with padded vinyl stools, circa 1970, the Reverend Wright stopped several times to exchange hugs with people who recognized him. Sitting at the far end of the bar was a man with a wireless microphone in his hand.

"Ladies and gentlemen," the man said over the public-address system, "I'm your host, Stan Davis, and I'm pleased to welcome to Lee's Unleaded Blues an honored guest—the Reverend Jeremiah..."—a long pause for effect—"WRIGHT!... pastor of Trinity United Church."

Several patrons let out loud whoops. When the noise subsided, Stan Davis went on:

"Pastor Wright, taught me this saying hisself: At Sunday church, everyone gets their lesson, but at Lee's Unleaded, it's time for their blessin'."

"Stan," the Reverend Wright said, "meet my friends, Vangie Roll and Alfie Douglas.

"Any friend of the Rev's."

"Stan's a retired police cop," the Reverend told us. "He's done some bodyguardin' for the Rolling Stones. Nobody messes with Stan."

Stan got up and escorted us to a table to the left, near the corner stage, which was called The Draw and where the acts performed. A pretty waitress, who introduced herself as Cookie, took our drink orders. I asked for club soda, and Vangie ordered a glass of white wine.

"Sweetness," the Reverend said to Cookie, "bring me a bottle of forty-year-old Glenfiddich. No ice, no soda, just a tall glass."

"I apologize, Reverend," Cookie said, "but Mr. Davis has given us strict instructions to inform customers how much certain drinks cost. And what you're ordering costs"— Cookie consulted a little pad that she held in her hand—"the forty-year-old Glenfiddich costs $3,813.99 a bottle."

"Don't worry your little head 'bout that, sweetness," the Reverend said. "Bring it on, bring it on!"

With that, he fished out a black American Express Centurion credit card and flipped it onto the table. I noted the raised lettering on the card: JEREMIAH WRIGHT, TRINITY UNITED CORPORATE EXPENSE ACCOUNT. It seemed he was spending on Barack Obama's credit a little early.

When the bottle of Glenfiddich came, the Reverend downed a full highball glass of the single-malt Scotch. He then refilled the glass, and downed *that* in a chugalug.

Before he had drained the last drop, a petite black woman approached our table. She wore an ornamental snood hairnet over the back of her head, fishnet stockings, and a clingy Diane von Furstenberg tie-front dress.

"Hi, Jerry," she said.

"Nailah Fonseca!" the Reverend said, feigning surprise. "Fancy meeting *you* here."

Nailah took a seat at our table just as Stan Davis appeared on The Draw and tapped the microphone to get everyone's attention.

"Ladies and Gentlemen, welcome to our Tribute to Muddy Night."

There was some applause.

"That's right. We have three acts, and all of 'em are playin' nuthin' but Muddy Waters tonight! First up is the Boogie Booker Quartet! Bring it on, Boogie!"

Four well-dressed young musicians—a drummer, bass player, guitar player and a pianist—took the stage. Boogie Booker, the lead singer, began the first song—"Hoochie Coochie Man."

The gypsy woman told my mother
Before I was born.

The place started going crazy. Feet were stomping and heads were bobbing and people were dancing and women were shimmying and everybody was having a great time. I looked over at the Reverend Jeremiah Wright, and he was having a great time, too. He and Nailah Fonseca were in a mean lip-lock.

"Come on, Jerry," Nailah Fonseca whispered. "Let's go to my place."

"Not yet," he said. "There's still plenty left in that bottle."

He emptied another four fingers' worth of Scotch into his glass. As he lifted the glass to his lips, though, it slipped from his fingers and spilled all over Nailah Fonseca's Diane von Furstenberg.

"Oh shee-*it!*" she cried. "I just bought this dress."

She jumped up and ran toward the ladies room.

"I'm shorry," the Reverend called after her. He was slurring his words.

This was the moment I had been waiting for.

"Reverend Wright," I said, "I was impressed by the way you handled that meeting at the church. And, frankly, I was surprised that you think Barack Obama can be elected president. Do you really think he's got a chance?"

The Reverend looked at me glassy-eyed, as though he hadn't understood what I said. I began to rephrase my question, but he raised his hand to stop me.

"If…if…if…he follows what I tell him—hell yes!" Wright replied. "It's all teed up for him. All's he got to do is follow the master plan."

He looked longingly at the bottle of Glenfiddich.

"Isn't the Clinton machine going to be tough to beat?" I asked. "After all, they basically own the Democrat Party."

"Alfie, before this thing...before it's over, the Clintons'll be yesterday's news. You'll see. Barack is The One."

The Boogie Booker Quartet was now singing "I'm Ready," and the room began to rock again. "Now I'm ready for you, I hope you're ready for me...."

As soon as the song ended, the Reverend took another drink and turned to me and asked, "So, Alfie, can I count on you?"

"Count on me for what?"

"To get CLIT to donate $250,000 to Trinity United?"

He sure had no problem being bold. I was starting to think I was in the wrong business. "Reverend, from what I saw earlier tonight, your operation is a money-generating machine. What do you need CLIT for?"

Jeremiah Wright clapped me on the shoulder. "Boy, there ain't ever enough money in this world."

Just then the Boogie Booker Quartet started playing another Muddy Waters song—"I Just Want to Make Love to You."

I don't want you to be my slave
I don't want you to work all day

When the song was over, the Reverend Wright picked up where he had left off.

"Alfie, you asked about Barack. Lemme tell you somethin'. He came to me....oh...almost twenty years ago. He was *Barry* Obama back then. Can you believe that? Callin' himself *Barry* when he possessed such a distinguished African name as Barack?"

I had to agree, Barry did sound goofy, but Barack? What kind of name was that? To my way of thinking, the child had more sense than the man.

"First thing I did was size the boy up," Wright continued. "Tall….nice lookin'…good teeth…datin' a nice woman…said he wanted to run for office…but he didn't have a clue about who *he* was! Alfie, that boy was *lost*! And he needed guidance…fatherly guidance. Most of all, *Barry* was searchin' for a father…and for a faith…and I gave both to him."

"Why was he looking for faith?" Vangie asked.

"I always suspected he was hidin' something' from me," the Reverend said. "His momma was an atheist, you know, and he never knew his real father, Barack Hussein Obama Sr., who was an African Muslim. So his stepfather, another Muslim fella named Lolo Soetero, raised him in Indonesia."

"Reverend," Vangie said, "are you saying that Barack Obama was a *Muslim* when he first came to see you?"

"Vangie," he said expansively, "I'm a Christian. I really don't care *what* he was before he stepped into Trinity United. Once he came to us, our job was to bring him to Christ."

"So how devout has he become?" Vangie asked.

The Reverend Wright chuckled. "Like other politicians. He uses the church as a prop. Makes a token financial contribution, and then makes sure the media knows about it. Shows up for a photo-op when the press is sniffin' around."

I felt it was time for me to jump into the conversation.

"Reverend," I said, "excuse me if I'm blunt, but if Senator Obama becomes President Obama, he'll be the front man, the salesman, the *draw* for Trinity United Church of Christ. The presence in your front pew of the President of the United States on Sundays will catapult your church onto the international stage. Your fundraising will go through the roof!"

The Reverend was nodding his head vigorously.

"So what else is new?" he said. "Why all the meetins? Why all the scripting of every word comin' out that boy's mouth? Hell, I even had to coach him on how to use a TelePrompTer from a podium. I've invested two decades in this project. Barack Obama isn't just like a son to me; he is my *creation*. You talk about that TV show, *Extreme Makeover*. Hell, I made over this future president. And I'll tell you one more thing. If there was any Muslim in that boy, I *washed* it all away."

The Reverend picked up Vangie's half-full glass of wine and downed it.

"Now, where's Nailah at?" he asked. "These women always disappearin' on me."

"She's over there at the bar," I said.

He stood up. He was unsteady on his feet and almost lost his balance. He grabbed the side of the table.

"Been a pleasure, Vangie. And Alfie, nice meetin' you, too. Please do your best getting' me that grant from CLIT."

With that, he stumbled over to the bar, gathered Nailah Fonseca, and the two of them disappeared into the smoky alcove leading to the front door.

Vangie and I remained silent for a moment.

Finally she said, "Higgy, are you thinking what I'm thinking?"

"Vangie, if Obama was once a Muslim—and if we can *prove* it—he's through. *Finished.* He isn't going to be president of anything."

She nodded her head in agreement.

"But *how* do we prove it?" she asked.

I stood up. "I'm taking our whole team—you, me, Russ, and Sydney Michael Green—to Indonesia."

CHAPTER TWENTY-SEVEN

During our grueling twenty-one-hour flight, Vangie Roll curled up next to me and slept with her head nestled on my shoulder. I tried that naval trick again, but she had a scoop neck that didn't give away nearly enough. Instead I watched Sidney Michael Green across the aisle, furiously pounding away on his laptop. From his occasional pointed looks at me, I was sure he was writing some slanderous report about my co-opting a fellow agent.

Our airplane touched down in the small port town of Banda Aceh (pronounced BAN-da AH-chay) on the tip of Sumatra, the westernmost island of the Indonesian archipelago. We had traveled halfway around the globe to the most devoutly Muslim city in the most populous Muslim country in the world to find a man none of us had ever heard of. Thanks to the ever-resourceful Russ Slanover, I had phone records proving that Barack Obama had recently been in touch with a mysterious Indonesian by the name of Badung Sabang.

I kept repeating the name in my mind. Compared to that, Barack Obama actually sound okay. What was it with all the kooky names, anyway?

After we landed, I tried to get some shuteye. But no sooner had I placed my head on the pillow than I heard my name being called.

"Higgy...Higgy...wake up!" Russ said. "There's been a massive earthquake deep under the Indian Ocean, one hundred miles from here. The energy it released is the equivalent of 23,000 Hiroshima-sized atomic bombs. It's uplifted the seabed, displacing vast amounts of seawater, and created a gigantic tsunami. The tsunami's headed...*here!*"

I threw on some clothes and went outside to the terrace of our CIA safe house, which was located on a hill high above Banda Aceh. Vangie Roll was already there, taking in the morning sunshine. She looked fresh and alluring in a short khaki skirt, a form-fitting white camisole, and a Chicago Cubs baseball cap.

"Hi, Higgy," she said, throwing her arms around my neck and pressing her tall, lean body against mine. "Give us a good-morning kiss."

I tried to avoid it, but her lips homed in on mine like a heat-seeking missile. And they were definitely giving off heat. If I wasn't...well, who I am...we'd be running right back inside.

Sydney Michael Green was at the other end of the balcony. He glanced over in our direction just in time to catch me trying to disentangle myself from Vangie's clinch. Oh, great, another item for his report. Then he averted his gaze and peered through a Celestron Astromaster 114 EQ Reflector Telescope that was pointed down at the town of Banda Aceh.

"What's going on down there?" I asked him, panting, finally breaking free.

"A lot of topless babes on the beach," Sydney Michael Green said. "All sizes, shapes, and colors."

"Oh, Syd, you're such an adolescent!" Vangie said.

"If you'd give me a chance, Vangie, I'd just as soon look through the telescope at you," Sydney Michael Green said. "Even with your clothes on, you're a lot sexier than those babes on the beach. But you're too busy making goo-goo eyes at Higgy…."

The early morning sky was a deeper and darker shade of blue than any sky I had never seen. There was a gentle, warm breeze coming off the Indian Ocean, but it was already stifling hot. Dozens of colorful birds were flying around in erratic patterns, making an unholy racket.

"Jesus H. Christ!" Sydney Michael Green said.

He was still looking through the telescope, and I assumed he had spotted more topless women.

"Will you look at *that*!" he said.

"Syd…." Vangie said.

But I detected a different tone in Sydney Michael Green's voice—one of shock and panic.

"What in God's name!" he shouted.

I walked over to the edge of the terrace and looked out to sea. A towering wave—nearly one hundred feet high—was sweeping toward the shore. At first, the people on the beach seemed awestruck. They stood there, hugging each other, staring wordlessly at the tsunami. Then, all at once, they grabbed their children and belongings and began running—back toward the tree line and the hills, desperately trying to reach higher ground.

But it was a race they could not win. The tsunami crashed over the beach, crushing everything in its path. The buildings near the beach were instantly obliterated. Then the wave kept moving into the more heavily forested areas. Huge trees snapped in half. The onrushing tsunami picked up a five-ton truck, tossed it against a two-story cinder-block building, and carried both truck and building away.

I was in a quandary what to do. Should I go down there and try to rescue some of the victims of the tsunami? Or should I use the disaster as "cover" for our mission—the hunt for Barack Obama's mysterious friend, Badung Sabang?

The wave stopped advancing. For a moment the water appeared to be still, and then it began receding with a great sucking sound. From our perch, we had a perfect view of the devastation that it left behind. We could see areas where man-made structures had stood five minutes ago. They were now completely swept clean. Only one building remained standing: a mosque in the middle of the town.

"Okay, here's the plan," I said. "Sydney Michael Green and I are going down there to see what we can do to help. Vangie, you and Russ go inland, pose as relief workers, and start looking for Badung Sabang. I have a hunch this disaster will flush him out."

Sydney Michael Green and I headed down the steep, winding road. We immediately ran into a mass of panicked survivors trudging up the hill. The tsunami had ripped off most of their clothing and left many of them seriously injured. Wails of anguish rose from the ranks of men, women, children, and old people.

We arrived at the village—or the place where the village had once stood—and stared in utter disbelief at the heaps of corpses washed up against building foundations and wedged between rocks. The few survivors stared at us in silence. There was almost no sound at all.

Then I heard a soft moan. It was a woman's voice.

"Kennedy!... Kennedy!...."

I stopped to listen and heard it again.

"Kennedy!..."

Above me, in the crook of a leafless tree, was a naked blonde. Her left leg was bent and twisted. I climbed up the tree and tried to dislodge her body. She cried out in pain.

"I'm here to help," I explained. "I'll try not to hurt you."

"Sie müssen aufhören!" she said.

Hearing that familiar German phrase—"You must cease!"—startled me. It brought back memories of making love to Taitsie in the lavatory of a flight from Frankfurt, while a German stewardess pounded on the door shouting *"Sie müssen aufhören!"*

As I lowered the naked blonde into the arms of Sydney Michael Green, she groaned in pain again. Her broken leg was already changing color to a light shade of purple.

Sydney Michael Green laid her on the ground. Her skin, which was deeply tanned except for the white outline of her missing bikini, was covered with pieces of seaweed. She was quite beautiful, tall and thin as a fashion model.

In the presence of so much beauty, Sydney Michael Green was uncharacteristically silent. There were no misogynistic wisecracks, no macho posturing. Instead, he looked down at the unfortunate woman with what could only be described as an expression of sorrow and compassion. Then he took off his shirt and wrapped it around her shoulders.

She moved her unbroken leg and I noticed that she was wearing a white gold ankle bracelet filled with diamonds and emeralds. If real—and it certainly *looked* real—this anklet was worth a fortune. This mysterious woman was not only beautiful; she was fabulously rich.

Her eyelashes fluttered and she slowly regained consciousness. She looked up at me and said something in German, which I didn't understand.

"Do you speak English?" I asked.

"*Ja*," she said in a weak voice. "Veer *ist mein* Kennedy?"

Sydney Michael Green carried the naked blonde tsunami victim up the hill to above our CIA safe house, where we found Vangie Roll. She was talking to a European doctor, who was in charge of a makeshift rescue area. Doctor Kitzel (as he was named) took one look at the woman in Sydney's arms, and rushed over to his side.

"Please," he said, "take the Countess to that empty tent."

"*Countess!*" Sydney Michael Green exclaimed. "Higgy, we rescued a real live countess!"

Inside the tent, Sydney Michael Green laid the Countess on a cot. Vangie spoke to her in German, and provided a running translation.

"She's Countess Gladys of Thurn und Taxis," Vangie said, "and she's from one of Europe's oldest and most prestigious families. She's a big jet-set celebrity. I remember reading about her in *Star* magazine."

"Veer *ist mien* Kennedy?"

"Who?" Vangie asked.

"*Mein* Chinese Crested accessory dog *ist namen* Kennedy. It goes *mit* me everywhere—to parties...movie premieres... orgies...."

"Why did you name him Kennedy?" I asked.

"Because Teddy Kennedy took me to Hyannisport and *shtupped* my brains out all weekend. And then he wouldn't even take my phone calls. So the least I could do was name my dog after him."

Just then Russ Slanover appeared in our tent. He was sweating and out of breath.

"Higgy, I have a lead on the guy we've been looking for," he said. "Badung Sabang."

"Where is he?"

"Not far from here. Just over the hill."

Countess Gladys moaned again, "Kennedy… Kennedy!"

I explained to Russ Slanover that the countess had lost her Chinese Crested accessory dog.

"That's strange," Russ said. "Because Badung Sabang is just up the hill, and he's rescuing dogs and cats."

As we prepared to leave Countess Gladys and follow Russ Slanover to the top of the hill, Sydney Michael Green pulled me aside.

"Higgy," he said, "I think I should stay behind and look after the Countess. I'll meet up with you and the rest of the team in Jakarta."

"This is no time for your usual monkey business," I said.

"I know this sounds strange, Higgy, but I have this *feeling* that I just want to *protect* her," he said.

I couldn't be sure whether Sydney Michael Green was being sincere, but I didn't care. If he wanted to absent himself from the interview with Badung Sabang and miss out on possibly crucial information that would sink the Obama ship forever, that was fine with me.

"I understand perfectly. You just stay right here."

CHAPTER TWENTY-EIGHT

A bright red Sikorsky S-92 preyed in the middle of a clearing, its rotor still spinning. I noticed the symbol on its side: a blue globe with the words INTERNATIONAL ANIMAL RESCUE. Nearby, a large makeshift pen contained a menagerie of animals—dogs, cats, a miniature donkey, and a goat or two.

Russ Slanover pointed out a tall, dark-skinned man with thick, wavy hair standing in the midst of a chaotic scene. The man was carrying a manila envelope stuffed with cash, and he was trying to hold back a group of shouting refugees, many of them barefoot and clothed in wrap-around skirts, and all of them desperate to leave Banda Aceh on the waiting helicopter.

"That's Badung Sabang," Russ Slanover told me. "He works for International Animal Rescue, an Indonesian charitable organization, but as you can see, he's hustling some cash on the side by charging exorbitant prices to evacuate people."

I nodded in approval at this impromptu display of capitalism. Simple supply and demand. “Okay,” I said, “let’s see what we can do.”

The three of us—Russ, Vangie, and I—approached Badung Sabang.

“We’re Americans,” I said. “We need to get to Jakarta as quickly as possible.”

Badung Sabang did a quick calculation in his head.

“Eight thousand U.S.,” he said.

Oh, so he wanted to bargain? “Maybe you’ll give us a special deal,” I said. ”We’ve heard that you went to school with Barack Obama. This lady here”—I pointed to Vangie Roll—“is a friend of Barack Obama’s from Chicago. They play basketball together.”

Badung Sabang was suitably impressed. “Barack—he’s going to be your next President.”

“Maybe, maybe not,” I said.

“Why not?” Badung Sabang asked.

“Because,” I said, “in America, some people believe the school you went to with Barack Obama, the Besuki School, was a Muslim madrassa, which would make Senator Obama a Muslim.”

Badung Sabang smiled as if he had been down this road before. “You need to talk to the imam.”

“Who?”

“Imam Selatin was very close to Barack,” Badung Sabang clarified. “He gave Barack private religious instruction. Go talk to him.”

"Do you know how we can find him?"

"Sure," Badung Sabang said, opening his arms wide. "He's my boss at the International Animal Rescue Foundation. You need to go to Jakarta and talk to him. But it'll cost you eight thousand dollars."

I knew this routine. "Four thousand," I countered.

He looked at me like I was the most foolish man in the world. "Eight. I'm not the one who has to go talk to the imam.

He had a point. Besides, it was only the taxpayers' money anyway. I reached into my pocket and took out the contingency "flash cash" I always carried for situations like this. I paid Badung Sabang his asking price, and he shoved the money into his manila envelope.

"Of course," Badung Sabang said, "before Imam Selatin can talk to you, he'll have to get permission from the Russian gentleman who *funds* the Animal Rescue Foundation."

I had a sinking feeling in my stomach. "That gentleman's name wouldn't happen to be Yurik Maligin, would it?"

"How did you know?" Badung Sabang asked.

"Just a lucky guess."

CHAPTER TWENTY-NINE

"Five days of nothing. No meetings…no returned phone calls… not even a sighting…."

I was venting my frustration to Russ Slanover. He was seated next to me on a metal bench in Jaya Ancol Park in Jakarta, overlooking the Pasar Seni art market. Since the arrival of the Tchaikovsky Circle in the Indonesian capital on December 27, we had failed in all our efforts to track down the mysterious Imam Selatin, who had tutored Barack Obama, or Barry Soetero as he was known when he was a young boy living in Indonesia with his mother and stepfather. Barack Obama, Barry Soetero, what was with all these strange names? We should have been able to hang him on that alone.

In any case, we had wasted five precious days, of my precious time, and now here it was, New Year's Day, 2006, and I had nothing positive to report to my boss, Whitney Nutwing.

I was a failure, and a little voice inside my head kept saying: *Who's the nutwing now?*

"It's not as bad as you're making it out, Higgy," Russ Slanover said, as though he had read my mind. "Look at it from a scientific point of view. Look at the profile we've developed on Imam Selatin."

Russ worked the keys on his high-tech laptop computer, and then twisted the screen so that I could see the results. I stared at an old, slightly out-of-focus black-and-white photo of Imam Selatin. The face that stared back at me had burning dark eyes, a long nose, and a graying beard. These prophets, I thought, really had to lose the beard.

"What's that's mark on the left side of the Imam's face?" I asked.

"A naevus flammeus nuchae," Russ answered.

"A *what?*"

"A port-wine stain birthmark. I found out the Imam has tried everything to get rid of it, including freezing, radiation, and the neodymium YAG laser." He didn't bother trying to explain that to me. "The behavioral profilers at Langley suspect that his facial birthmark—his *disfigurement*—has a lot to do with the Imam's embittered, *blood*thirsty nature."

"He carries the mark of Cain."

"That's the wrong religion," Russ said. "But you *could* say that the Imam's private Islamic school—his madrassa—reflects his authoritarian, fundamentalist nature. The school teaches the Wahhabi form of Islam, which encourages violence against Jews and Christians and moderate Muslims. The school preaches that Western-style democracy is responsible for all the world's ills, and that Osama bin Laden will cure those ills with sword and fire."

"Not exactly a liberal-arts curriculum," I observed. "Where is the Greek? Where is the Latin?".

He ignored the outburst. "The weird part is that the Imam's school is partnered with International Animal Rescue. It teaches its students basic veterinarian skills," Russ continued. "The financial forensics experts at Langley have traced the funding for the school to your old adversary, Yurik Maligin."

"That's all fine and good," I said, "but what I want to know is why Maligin is funding an obscure Muslim imam here in Jakarta."

"That," said Russ Slanover, "is still the sixty-four-thousand rupiah question." He seemed very pleased with himself, but I wasn't impressed. At 9,000 rupiahs to the dollar, that made it roughly the seven-dollar question. The world wasn't craning its neck to find out the answer to that.

New Year's Day was a national holiday and the Pasar Seni art market was packed with families inspecting handicrafts and souvenirs from all over Indonesia. The sight of these parents with their children made me wish that I was back home with Vier instead of chasing an elusive imam. These children resurrected all my nagging doubts about my priorities.

True, my work for the Tchaikovsky Circle was of vital importance. Trying to protect the CIA—and thus the United States itself—from immoral, miscreant politicians was a worthy cause. But so, too, was trying to raise Vier in a happy home environment. I had already lost Taitsie who, until Vier was born, was the most important person in my life. Our marriage was shattered because of my long, unexplained absences. No other woman could ever capture my heart the way Taitsie had. Without her, I had a huge, gaping hole in my soul. Only being back with her and Vier could make my life whole again. But how could I ever begin to restore my family if I was over here in Jakarta, or in a dozen other places where this Barack Obama assignment took me?

A ring on my cell phone interrupted my musings. I recognized the distinctive sound announcing a call from Vangie Roll—Billie Holiday singing "God Bless the Child."

"What do you have?" I asked.

"Imam Selatin's secretary blew me off," Vangie said. "She said the Imam was out on a Russian yacht and wouldn't be back for an indefinite period of time."

"So Maligin is one step ahead of us—*again*!"

"Don't despair," Vangie said. "I think I've found a way to infiltrate the imam's circle. His ex-daughter-in-law lives nearby. She had a bitter divorce from the imam's son, and under Muslim law, she lost custody of their children."

"Why would she talk to us—total strangers?" I asked.

"I told her you were the president of the Sticky Fingers Literary Agency," Vangie said, "and that I was one of your writers. I am supposedly doing research for a book on renowned Asian Islamic teachers, including Imam Selatin. The ex-daughter-in-law, Gema Darmadi—that's her name—invited us for tea. Higgy, she sounds like a lonely, scorned woman who needs someone to spill all her beans to."

The imagery sounded grotesque, but I merely said, "Pick me up in a taxi and we'll go see her."

Less than an hour later, Vangie and I arrived by taxi at a modest two-story house in the Kebayoran Baru residential section of Jakarta. A tall woman in her early forties greeted us at the door. She was dressed in a relaxed white cotton pantsuit, a wide red belt, and gold slippers. Her dark hair was swept up and pinned back, revealing a long, elegant neck. I wanted to make like a swan with her, but I had a duty to do.

"Welcome, Miss Roll and Mr. Higginbothem," she said in a pronounced accent. "I'm Gema Darmadi and it is a delight to meet you."

Gema Darmadi led us onto a bright screened porch, where a traditional English tea service and a small angel food cake awaited us. We sat on wicker chairs. I detected the intoxicating smell of aloe incense sticks burning in bamboo holders.

"Mr. Higginbothem, how do you prefer your tea?"

"Just with lemon, please."

I noticed that she didn't put any sugar in her tea and didn't touch the piece of cake in front of her. No wonder she kept her girlish figure.

She looked at Vangie and then at me. "So, you two are in love."

I almost spat up a mouthful of tea.

"I can tell," Gema Darmadi said. "You two have a shared destiny."

"A shared *what*?" I said.

Gema Darmadi had a dreamy look on her face.

"A shared destiny, Mr. Higginbothem, is what we all strive for. To go through life with a partner on an equal footing."

Vangie was nodding her head vigorously.

I decided this line of conversation was getting out of hand.

"Our *destiny* is to learn more about your former father-in-law," I said.

The faraway look hardened into sharp lines. Hell truly has no wrath like a woman scorned.

"I have known Imam Selatin since I was a child," she began. "His son, Suki, and I were childhood friends who later fell in love. My parents and his parents were social friends and they approved of our marriage. We were married in 1979, when both of us were eighteen years old. We had three children together. And we were divorced seven years ago."

She stopped, and for a moment she seemed ready to cave in.

Vangie and I looked at each other. What malignant, desperate secret had we unearthed now?

"The situation in the imam's house, where we lived, was not…*proper*," she said, "and I could not live that way anymore." Her eyes began to tear up. "I'm sorry…all this reminds me of the suffering I endured…"

We gave her all the time she needed to recover. This was getting juicy. Then she said, "Imam Selatin told me that since I had attended a Christian missionary school, I needed to be taught how to be a good Muslim wife. I had to allow him to teach me how to be a proper Muslim woman in the bedroom."

"What did *that* mean?" Vangie asked.

"He tried to *rape* me," Gema Darmadi exclaimed. "And he told me that if I tried to protest, Allah would judge me a failed Muslim."

She paused again and dabbed at her eyes with a tissue.

"He chased me around and around the house," she continued. "Around and around until he started getting dizzy. That's when I kicked him in the shin and told him what a dirty, filthy old creep he was."

Vangie looked aghast. "Did you tell your husband?"

"I did," Gema answered. "I couldn't hide it. Yet Suki put all the blame on me. To tell the truth, if it wasn't his father, it looked like he wanted to do a three-way."

Vangie and I remained silent at this shocking news. Could anyone imagine doing a three-way with a man who had a gross beard like that?

I coughed, trying to dispel the somber mood that had fallen over us. "Gema, I'm sorry for bringing up the painful past," I said. "But as Miss Roll told you, we're researching a book on Islamic teachers. Our American audience would be fascinated by how Imam Selatin tutored an American boy. There is the case of Barry Soetero, for example."

Her eyes lit with sly understanding. "Yes," she said. "Nowadays, he calls himself Barack Obama. I heard bonny Barry will be your next President."

She sipped her tea, and the shadow of a smile came over her tear-stained face.

"There's a story about that case," she said. "Before the divorce, Imam Selatin told Suki and me that his mission—'My greatest mission for Allah,' the filthy old creep called it—was to take young foreign boys living here in Indonesia and convert them to Islam. Every year he took on another one—French, English, German…specially selected from local schools—but only one American in all those years."

"Was this Imam Selatin's idea?" I asked.

"No," Gema Darmadi said. "The dirty old creep told Suki and me that he was part of an organization called the International Council for Allah. They meet once a year in Cairo and review their progress in training young boys. They send the boys back to their home countries to grow up and enter government and politics. Later, the boys are called on to do their duty."

"Duty?" I said, startled by this new turn.

"Yes," Gema said, "their duty to help reestablish the historic Caliphate—rule by Islamic clerics—that dominated the Muslim world until five hundred years ago. "

I listened in stunned silence. Was there really a Muslim plan to recruit, indoctrinate, and plant converted Muslims inside non-Muslim governments with the hope that they would someday rise to hold high governmental positions? As outlandish as this sounded, the scheme resembled Soviet plans during the Cold War to train Communist sleeper agents, and then plant them in foreign countries for future activation.

"Gema," I said, "what can you tell us about Barry Soetero? What do you recall about him and the imam?"

"Oh, I remember the day Barry graduated from the perverted old creep's tutorship," she replied. "Suki and I were about the same age as Barry—about seven years old—and the wicked old creep invited us to the festive occasion of Barry's *Khitan*, the term for male circumcision carried out as an Islamic rite.

"There were dozens of politicians and businessmen with their wives," she went on. "Everyone was dressed up. All this happened more than thirty years ago, but I remember it as if it was yesterday. Barry was a very quiet and polite boy. He always seemed distant and detached. He didn't have many friends. Just one—a boy named Badung Sabang. But that day Barry acted very nervous, because the disgusting old creep said he wanted to test him in front of everyone."

"Test him? How?" I asked.

"To see if he had learned his lessons. So the disturbed old creep gathered everyone around in the big living room on prayer mats. There were several visiting imams. And the muTahhir—he's the man who does the Muslim circumcision—he was preparing his table in the back of the room. The warped old creep made Barry kneel on a prayer mat in front of everyone and answer questions."

"What kind of questions?"

"Like, 'Barry, who is responsible for the spread of imperialism?'"

"How did he respond?"

"Barry knew the answer right away. 'The United States of America is responsible for the spread of imperialism,' he said."

I wanted to shake her hand. "What else did the imam ask him?"

"He asked, "Barry, what should a good American do about this?'"

"What did he say?"

"He said, 'Apologize for it.' All the grown-ups applauded! Several of them praised the deviant old creep for being such a good tutor. The creepazoid and his wife were beaming. So he said, 'Barry, as the final test please show our guests here how you, as an American, should properly greet a foreigner.'

"Barry got up from his prayer mat, walked in front of the grown-ups, and slowly bowed—very, very deeply—and held the position for the longest time before standing back up straight. And the debauched old creep said, 'Barry is the best bower I have ever coached!'

"At this point the muTahhir took Barry to a table in the back of the room and had him lie on it," Gema went on. "Everyone gathered around as he pulled Barry's pants down and did a quick circumcision. He handed the foreskin to the pedophiliac old creep, who said to the group, 'By this act, we have completed the Covenant with Abraham and we have cleansed Barry of his impure American ideas. We now welcome young Barry Soetero into the ranks of Allah's children.' "

Gema began laughing.

Vangie asked, "What's so funny? I don't see *anything* funny about that."

"As the nefarious old creep was holding up Barry's foreskin and speaking," Gema said, "Java, my dog, jumped up and grabbed it and ran off with it. Suddenly, thirty adults were knocking over tables and drinks as my dog ran around with Barry's foreskin hanging from his mouth."

"Did your dog *eat* the foreskin?" I asked, fascinated.

"No, my mother-in-law elbowed her way through the crowd, sending people flying in all directions, and tackled Java and pried the foreskin out of his mouth," Gema said. "The unsavory old creep put it in a jar and labeled it. I think he still keeps it as a trophy in his office."

CHAPTER THIRTY

"Did you believe Gema Darmadi about the foreskin?" Sydney Michael Green asked doubtfully the next day. "And how about the imam saving that foreskin all these years in his office?"

"I don't know," I said. "It isn't the CIA's standard operating procedure to rely on a sawed-off piece of the human anatomy."

"Well," Sydney Michael Green said, "there's only one way to find out."

"What's that?" I automatically distrusted any brilliant ideas of his.

"Break into the imam's office and find Barack Obama's foreskin."

"O-kay."

I wasn't eager to follow Sydney Michael Green's advice about conducting a break-in. And for a good reason. Shortly after I joined the CIA, my father told me that he'd been up to his eyeballs in the botched CIA break-in of the Democratic National Committee headquarters at the Watergate complex back in the

1970s. Only the last-minute intervention of his old friend Bill Casey saved The Deuce from being indicted as a Watergate co-conspirator and sent to the Maxwell Correctional Facility in Alabama.

"Higgy," the Deuce had told me, "I learned an important lesson from Watergate and I want to pass it on to you. You can lie and cheat for the CIA—that's fine. You can ruin other people's reputations—okey-dokey. You can betray and double-cross your friends—all's fair in love and war. You can terminate America's adversaries with extreme prejudice—no sweat. But Higgy, listen to me: never, *ever* EVER! get involved in some two-bit break-in of an office building in the middle of the night."

It crossed my mind that Sydney Michael Green might be setting me up—and that *this* two-bit break-in in Jakarta could be his way of discrediting me and taking over the Tchaikovsky Circle. Nevertheless, in the dead of night on January 3, 2005, the two of us broke into the top floor of the Wisma Tower, the tallest building in downtown Jakarta.

My flashlight swept across the marble floor and polished walnut walls until it came to rest on a modern san serif logo:

International Animal Rescue Foundation

"Higgy, this way!" Sydney Michael Green whispered.

I followed him down a corridor adorned with photos of rescued animals until we came to Imam Selatin's corner office.

Inside, floor-to-ceiling windows framed a spectacular view of nighttime Jakarta.

"Quick, over here!" Sydney Michael Green whispered. "Look!"

He was standing in front of a huge cabinet made of the same polished walnut wood used in the entrance. The cabinet had twenty-six slots marked by modern san serif letters—one for each letter in the English alphabet. And each of the slots held one or more jars containing foreskins preserved in formaldehyde.

"Here's a jar under the letter 'A' with a French name—'Jean-Louis Auteuil,' " Sydney Michael Green said. "There's a German name under 'B'—'Hans Bruhl.' "

"Look under' O' for 'Obama,' " I said.

"Sydney Michael Green checked and said, Nothing's under 'O.'"

"How about 'S' for 'Soetero'? "

"Nothing," he said. "Hey, wait a minute. I see something! There's a stain."

"What kind of stain?" I asked.

"The kind of stain that a glass leaves on a wood table."

"Let me see," I said.

And sure enough, there was a stain.

"Hand me a jar," I told Sydney Michael Green.

I placed the jar over the mark in the empty slot for 'S'.

"It fits perfectly," I said. "There was a jar here before. But now it's missing because somebody has taken it."

Sydney Michael Green stepped back and whispered, "Jesus, Higgy, look at *this*!"

He was staring at a framed photograph hanging on the wall above the counter. I shone my flashlight on it and saw a color picture of Imam Selatin and Yurik Maligin toasting each other with a vial just like the ones we were searching for. The signed, handwritten caption from Maligin to the Imam, read, "On to the Oval Office!"

Sidney Michael Green turned to me with a shrewd smile. "It looks like you've been topped again."

"Drat it!"

CHAPTER THIRTY-ONE

A week later, I was making French toast and Jimmy Dean sausages for my nine-year-old son, Vier. He was staying with me as per the every-other-weekend custody visitation plan that Taitsie and I had worked out in our separation agreement.

When the French toast was ready, I called upstairs, "Vier, come on down, breakfast is ready."

As I piled the golden pieces of French toast on a chafing dish, a shaft of wintry sunlight fell through the kitchen window of my home on M Street in Georgetown. The old white clapboard house had once belonged to my mother, and when she died, she left it to my sisters and me. But both of them lived abroad—Faith in Neuilly, outside Paris, with her third Saudi husband, and Hope on her never-ending – and very expensive – obsessive search for the remains of Amelia Earhart. The last I had heard, Hope was encamped on a small atoll near Palau in the South Pacific, along with a hut filled with scuba-diving equipment. I had bought out my sisters' shares in the family home and made this my base. This was where Taitsie and I had lived until she left me. Some of her clothes were still upstairs in her closet.

"*Breakfast!*" I called again.

Suddenly, Vier flew through the kitchen door and slid halfway across the black-and-white tiled floor. He was wearing a vintage 1950s flowered shirt, which he had bought with his allowance on rustyZipper.com, and his hair was combed in a mop that pointed straight at the ceiling. Two weeks before, he and I had watched an episode of *Seinfeld*, and this morning, Vier was doing his Cosmo Kramer imitation, complete with a pair of trousers that fell two inches short of his loafers.

He leaned over the chafing dish and took a melodramatic sniff.

"French toast and sausages!" he said. "Giddy-up!"

"Vier," I said, checking my watch, "we're going to be late for your art class. Eat your breakfast."

Vier shoved a huge piece of French toast into his mouth. As a dollop of maple syrup coursed down his chin, I suppressed the urge to criticize my son's bad manners. Instead, as a distraction, I clicked on the old thirteen-inch kitchen TV set, and after a few seconds, Katie Couric appeared on the screen. She was interviewing Senator-elect Barack Obama as they walked in front of the Capitol.

Katie was wearing black high heels and a short skirt cut on the bias to mid-thigh, which showed off her short, stubby legs. Her tight sleeveless white blouse emphasized her substantial bosom. Her hair was dyed blonde and cut pixie short. But Obama's eyes were focused on one thing—her fleshy upper arms.

"Dad," Vier said, "look at her high beams!"

My son was right: Katie's erect nipples were clearly visible through her blouse. She was in full swoon over Barack Obama.

"Senator," Katie said, "you've been quoted as saying that you won't run for president in 2008. But what if I told you that we in the media *need* you to save this country? Could we convince you to run?"

Obama flashed a toothy smile but didn't say a word.

"Senator," Katie pressed on, "there are times in American history when one man comes along and rescues us all. Lincoln did it. FDR did it. And now it's *your* turn. Only *you* can rescue us from the ravages of the greedy Republicans and the crazy, racist conservatives. Only you can rescue my evening news show from its declining Nielsen ratings."

Obama was still smiling – and still staring at Katie's arms. Finally, he spoke up.

"Katie," he said, "do you want to know what I really think?"

"By all means," she said, leaning forward.

"Everything's George W. Bush's fault. Everything, that is, except your ratings."

CHAPTER THIRTY-TWO

My BlackBerry started vibrating like a Mexican jumping bean, rousing me from a deep sleep.

For more than two years now, I had been traveling the world searching for the truth about Barack Obama, and in the early morning darkness of yet another hotel room, it took me a moment to orient myself. Where was I? Then I remembered: I was in Chicago's Ambassador East, where Joe Kennedy had conspired with Sam Giancana to make JFK president of the United States. I fumbled around the bedside table and caught the phone on its fourth ring.

"Hello," I croaked, still half asleep.

"Higgy, you've got no business sleeping. You think James Bond sleeps? You think Jack Bauer sleeps? You think the Pink Panther sleeps?"

There was no mistaking the voice of Vangie Roll's mother.

"What time is it?"

"After midnight," she said.

"Elvira, for Christ's sakes, what do you want at this hour?"

"Listen, today's Friday. Tomorrow, Obama's going to make a formal announcement that he's running for president. At the Old State Capitol in Springfield, where Abe Lincoln did his thing. Vangie just got a call from the Reverend Jeremiah Wright telling her that he's going to give the public invocation. He invited Vangie and me as his personal guests. And he asked if you—*you* being Alfie Douglas, who controls all that CLIT money—if you'd care to come along. Of course, if you think your beauty sleep's more important...."

The next day, the Reverend Wright's chauffeur, Malcolm, picked us up at Vangie's house in the Hyde Park section on the South Side of Chicago. And three hours later, as Malcolm maneuvered his limo into a reserved parking space near the Old State Capitol Building in Springfield, Illinois, I could hear the chant of the crowd:

"Obama! Obama! Obama!"

It was Saturday morning, February 10, 2007, a teeth-chattering seven degrees, and yet nearly twenty thousand people were packed into the town square. There was enough media on hand to cover the Normandy invasion.

Malcolm and I helped Elvira into her wheelchair. Then the four of us skirted the edge of the crowd and ducked into an elevator that carried us down to an underground command center outfitted with high-tech equipment. All the members of Barack Obama's brain trust were there: the Reverend Wright; Valerie Jarrett, who was Michelle and Barack Obama's closest friend;

the former Weatherman William Ayres and his wife, Bernardine Dohrn; and Van Jones, who thought that 9/11 was a put-up job by the United States government. Nothing seemed to have changed in all this time. At least I *thought* nothing had changed until I saw the purplish flush on the Reverend Wright's face. He was absolutely livid.

"What's the matter, pastor?" I asked. "You look like somebody stole the collection plate."

"Barack pulled the invitation for me to give the public invocation," he said. "Fifteen minutes before Shabbos—that's sundown Friday night—I got a call from Barack. Some pussies on his staff talked him into *un*inviting me because of the things I've been saying."

"What things?" Elvira said.

"Like, racism is how this country was founded and how this country is still run," he replied. "Like, we in this country believe in white supremacy and black inferiority and believe it more than we believe in God." He was working himself up, as though he was delivering a pulpit-thumping sermon. "Like, we care nothing about human life if the ends justify the means. Like, God has got to be sick of this shit!"

"Oh, *those* things," Elvira said. "Lordy, I can't imagine why a brother running for president of the United States would want to distance himself from such cheerful and heartwarming sentiments."

Just then Valerie Jarrett approached.

"Jerry," she said, putting her arm around the Reverend Wright's shoulder, "I know how bad you must feel about not being able to give the benediction. But you've got to put aside your hurts because frankly things aren't going well for our boy. Just look at him."

Valerie Jarrett pointed through a doorway leading to an adjoining room. There, standing at a replica of the outdoor stage above us, complete with a podium and TelePrompTer, was Senator Barack Obama, practicing his announcement speech. Was it my imagination, or had he grown a beard? A beard just like....

"I don't feel any *energy* coming from him," Valerie Jarrett told the Reverend Wright. "There's no spark. He's remote. An ethereal presence. One minute he's there, the next he's not. Jerry, I'm telling you—you've got to *do* something!"

The Reverend Wright smiled broadly. Finally, something to do. "Okay, I know how to fix this," he said, ducking into the next room.

The Reverend Wright stopped Obama in mid-sentence. "Barack, take off that beard!"

The younger man looked reluctant but gave in. With one swipe, the uncanny resemblance to Abe Lincoln was gone.

Then the Reverend Wright turned to the floor director. "Sammy," he said, "start the metronome! And give me a nice slow fifteen beats a minute—one every four seconds."

Suddenly, the room was filled with the *tick...tick...tick* beat of a metronome.

"Barack," the Reverend said, "on each beat you switch from the left TelePrompTer screen to the right screen. That way you look like you're not reading but you're speaking directly to the audience."

Obama nodded.

"Not just to hold an office, but..." Obama read, looking at the left TelePrompTer. Then, on the beat of *four*, he turned, rather stiffly, and continued from the right TelePrompTer: "... but to gather with you to transform a nation."

He read it calmly. Dispassionately. And he followed the beat of the metronome. He said, "Not just to hold an office, but to transform a nation" over and over again—all to the *tick... tick...tick* beat of the metronome—while he shifted his head left and then right and then back to the left again.

The metronomic Obama was an improvement over the stiff and stilted Obama. But I could see that the Reverend Wright was still unhappy with the performance.

"Barack," Wright said, approaching the podium, "where's your *passion*? We're going to take care of this—this *passion* problem right now. Sammy," he called to the floor director, "bring in the backup group!"

A moment later, three black men dressed in tuxedos and three black women in shiny silver mini-dresses entered the room. They took positions at microphones behind Obama. One of the men looked familiar to me, but I couldn't place him.

"Barack," the Reverend said, "behind you is Boogie Booker and some backup singers that I brought over from Motown Records to help us out. They're going to *sing* the speech as you *speak* it. That way you're going to get some *lilt* in your delivery. Boogie Booker here is going to sing the lead—right along with you—and you just read it."

Now I suddenly recalled that Boogie Booker had played Muddy Waters songs at Lee's Unleaded Blues on the night Vangie and I had gone out drinking with Jeremiah Wright.

"Okay," the Reverend said, "let's take it from the top...on *three*. And *one* and *two* and *three*...."

The *tick...tick...tick* of the metronome began again. Obama started reading from the TelePrompTer, and Boogie Booker and the backup singers started snapping their fingers and swaying back and forth and singing the speech along with him.

Obama recited:

> As Lincoln organized the forces arrayed against slavery, he was heard to say: 'Of strange, discordant, and even hostile elements, we gathered from the four winds, and formed and fought to battle through.'

And Boogie Booker and the chorus sang:

> ...we gathered from the four winds, oh, yeah, and formed and fought to battle through... Oh, yeah....oh, yeah....

Obama's head was beginning to move rhythmically to the beat, and his voice was beginning to soar, and he was speaking in the hypnotic cadence of a Pentecostal preacher. He raised his chin and said loud and clear:

> That is our purpose here today!

And the back-up singers chimed in:

> ...Tell it, brother!

And Obama said:

> That's why I'm in this race. Not just to hold an office, but to gather with you to *transform a nation....*

And Boogie Booker sang out:

> Oh, yeah.... We've seen the Promised Land....

The candidate and his words had crystallized into a single, powerful, inspiring, perfect message. And I could feel the goose bumps go up my leg. I had discovered the secret remedy that could cure every mind-numbing speech given by all the brain-locked millionaires in Washington. They just needed a little bit of soul.

As Obama finished his run-through, everyone exploded in applause. The candidate stepped down from the practice podium and stopped in front of our small group. The room was suddenly suffused with the warm glow of his electrifying smile. He shook hands with each one of us, and then bent down to kiss Elvira on the cheek.

"Thanks for coming today, Miss Roll," he said. "I hope to see you again next Sunday at Trinity United Church."

"I'm there every Sunday," she said. "Wouldn't miss it."

"I've been there every Sunday for the past twenty years," Obama said proudly.

Then, suddenly, Obama did a quick double take when he saw Vangie Roll. A flicker of recognition crossed his face. Did he remember their basketball game more than two years earlier, or was it just the sight of an attractive woman? He said a few words to Vangie, and went to a corner and lit a cigarette.

"Elvira, come and sit over here with me," said the Reverend Wright. "We have a few minutes before the festivities begin."

He wheeled Elvira over to a sitting area. Valerie Jarrett, Vangie and I followed. We settled into chairs around a coffee table.

"Well," the Reverend said, "this morning is the beginning of Stage Two. We have won the Invisible Primary."

"Invisible Primary?" I said.

"Almost thirty years ago," the Reverend said, "Arthur T. Hadley, an editor at the old New York *Herald-Tribune,* wrote about the 1976 presidential campaign and how a complete nobody named Jimmy Carter came along and won something that Hadley called the Invisible Primary, which is *everything* that goes on *before* New Hampshire. Whoever is ahead in this invisible contest goes on to win the nomination and then the presidency. And our plan to win this Invisible Primary has worked. Barack is already ahead of Hillary and John Edwards. Just look at that crowd out there and all these reporters trying to suck up to him! The entire media establishment is in the bag for Barack."

"Five minutes!" an advance man yelled.

The candidate was still in the corner, talking to Valerie. Mrs. Obama and the girls appeared in their heavy winter coats. "Barack!" she commanded, and he looked up. "No more arms. You've got a speech to give."

"Oh, yes, of course," he said, rising to his feet. "A speech that'll make them love me. Love me, all of them, do you hear? All across the nation, all across the oceans, all across the whole wide—"

"Barack, come on!"

CHAPTER THIRTY-THREE

On the way back from Springfield, I received a text message on my BlackBerry. It was from my son Vier.

> Hi Dad. Glad you're back from your travels. I'm going to enter a talent contest at the Improv comedy club in D.C.
>
> How's this for my opening joke? One night as a couple lays down for bed, the husband starts rubbing his wife's arm. The wife turns over and says, "I'm sorry, honey, I've got a gynecologist appointment tomorrow and I want to stay fresh." The rejected husband thinks for a minute then taps his wife again. "Do you have a dentist appointment tomorrow, too?"
>
> By the way, Dad, Mom's having her first one-woman sculpture show Feb 22 here in NY.... Can U come? We'd be a family again. Please! Xox. V

That pitiful phrase—"We'd be a family again"—tugged at my heartstrings. Like all children of broken homes, Vier had fantasies that his mother and father would get back together.

I shared his dream. Indeed, I wanted to reconcile with Taitsie more than anything in the world. I loved her more now than I did on the day I married her. This separation was her idea, not mine—and it was killing me.

I suffered from what Winston Churchill called "the Black Dog"—that depressed state of mind where waking up and facing another day is almost unbearable. Getting out of bed took enormous effort; my arms felt as though they weighed a hundred pounds. Once awake, I was tormented by the same recurring thoughts: What could I have done to save our marriage? How could I tell Taitsie that it was *my* fault? And worst of all, who was Taitsie sleeping with?

As I knew all too well, Elizabeth "Taitsie" Millard was a sensual woman. I had no doubts that she was back on the dating scene in New York, a paradise for singles, divorcees and *separatees*. The thought of Taitsie—*my* Taitsie—indulging her libertine impulses with another man was too much for me to bear.

Taitsie and I hadn't seen each other in a long time. Occasionally, we talked on the phone about Vier. But otherwise, we were separated by a cold, long-distance silence. Now, reading Vier's text message, I began to wonder if Taitsie might be having second thoughts. Was *she* behind Vier's invitation to me to attend her one-woman show in New York? Was this a face-saving way for Taitsie to see if we could reconcile? Or was I indulging in wishful thinking?

I text-messaged Vier:

> I'll gladly come to NY for your Mother's show. Assume you want me to stay with you and your Mother in the apartment while in NY. I can use the guest room. Love Dad

Less than a minute later, Vier replied.

> Great news you're coming to NY. But I don't recommend you stay in the guest room at Mom's place. No way. Xox V

Why didn't Vier want me to stay in his Mother's apartment? Was he trying to protect me from something—or somebody? Was there another man in Taitsie's life?

Well, whether Vier liked it or not, I decided that I was going to stay in Taitsie's guest room and find out what this was all about.

CHAPTER THIRTY-FOUR

"Champagne?"

A waitress in a short black skirt and colorful Christian Lacroix stockings offered me a tray with glasses of champagne, sparkling water, and wine. I had been sober for four years, seven months, and thirteen days, and although I was nervous over the prospect of facing Taitsie again, I had no intention of having a slip now. So I took a glass of sparkling water.

It was a chilly Thursday night in SoHo, just off Gansevoort Street at the Eros & Agape Gallery. The gallery was one big, long rectangular room with stark white walls, a black ceiling, and a big window looking out on Little West 12th Street. It was crammed with Page Six boldfaced names from the worlds of art, society, and media. Flora Biddle, the former chairman of the Whitney Museum, was chatting up the painter Chuck Close. Caroline Kennedy was in an animated (one might even say "heated") conversation with her heavyset husband, Edwin Schlossberg, a designer of museum installations. Mayor Michael Bloomberg was steering his lanky investment banker girlfriend

Diana Taylor around the room. Richard Johnson, the guiding genius behind the *New York Post's* famous "Page Six," was in a corner schmoozing Tony Frost, the editor of the *National Enquirer....*

Among the many attractive women, two in particular caught my attention. They looked like twins: majestic, shapely, and with skin the color of the desert at sunset. Their bare arms and legs were incredibly long and limber. They stood together and shared a laugh. Their raw, natural beauty took my breath away.

"Dad, you came!"

Vier was dressed in a tie and jacket, though his shirttail was hanging out. With his glossy black hair and heavy straight eyebrows, he resembled his mother more than ever.

"Hey," Vier said, grabbing my wrist, "we gotta find Mom. She's here somewhere."

I looked around the crowded room and caught a glimpse of the fabulous, breathtaking, amazing Taitsie. She was taller than all the other women in the room, including the two majestic Desert Girls with whom she was talking.

"Have you seen Mom's sculptures?" Vier asked.

"Not yet," I said. "Why don't we take a look around together?"

Vier and I approached a small sculpture mounted on a table. It was entitled "Gobi" and depicted a tall, thin woman, seated, legs wide apart, head down. I frowned slightly. All of Taitsie's subjects had one thing in common: they were tall, thin, naked women. This piece made it appear that the woman was examining herself. I wondered if the model used for "Gobi" was one of the Desert Girls.

The next work was a full-sized piece of two women, arm-in-arm, staring off at some faraway object. The label attached to the wall next to it read "Shared Destiny." The two women were, as usual, thin and beautiful and nude.

"Sir, would you like a program?"

A gallery staffer was handing out Eros & Agape fliers. The cover read: VAGINAL ART 2007. ELIZABETH MILLARD.

Taitsie had kept her maiden name as her professional name. I couldn't blame her. Long before I met her, she had established a name for herself in the art world—a world that was as distant as you could get from my secret world at the CIA. However, in my *other* world—the world of my cover as the head of the Sticky Fingers Literary Agency—our two universes sometimes intersected. For instance, I had once pitched a book idea to Philippe Vergne, the senior curator of the Walker Art Center, to write the history of Neo-Avant-Garde. But Vergne declined the offer, explaining that it would "distract me from myself."

As Vier and I moved from sculpture to sculpture, I spotted George Soros, the enormously successful money speculator who was the chief backer of every left-wing cause du jour. He was wearing a blue *Obama 2008* button.

I sidled up to him as he studied another of Taitie's pieces, this one titled "Eritrea." The sculpture was a variation on

Taitsie's usual theme. It depicted two women *partially* dressed. Rags hung from their skeletal figures.

"It's sad about all the human misery in Eritrea, isn't it?" I said to Soros. "And all the suffering throughout the rest of Africa."

He grunted without looking at me.

So I tried again. "And it's about time we had an African-American president."

"Excuse me," Soros said, "but have we met?"

I smiled in my most innocent manner. "I'm the artist's husband, Theodore J. Higginbothem III."

"You've got to be kidding," he said.

"No, that's my real name," I said. "And this is my son, Vier."

As we shook hands, Soros looked me in the eye. He had what The Deuce called a "dour countenance." But my reference to Barack Obama and his African background seemed to have roused his interest.

"Yes, I believe Obama will be a transformational president," Soros said.

"You really think he can beat Hillary—and *Bill*?"

"I know Bill," Soros said with a deep insider's gravity, "and he's conflicted about Hillary. He only *half* wants his wife to win the nomination. His ego wants the Clinton brand to own the Democratic Party. But his vanity wants there to be only one president with the last name Clinton."

"Do you think the economy will help or hurt Obama?" I asked.

"The American economy is a house of cards," Soros replied even more loftily. "All it would take is one shrewd play to take down Lehman Brothers and the rest of the big banks. A collapse like that would help Barack Obama win the election."

"Is that so?" I said, playing along.

"That is *definitely* so. Believe me, I know whereof I speak, Mr. Higginbothem."

I could see Soros was forgetting himself as he pontificated about a subject close to his heart—money.

"And," he continued, "you're looking at the very man who can do it—make that play to take down the big banks and ensure that Barack Obama wins the White House. As they say, Mr. Higginbothem, stay tuned."

"I surely will," I said.

After George Soros left, Vier tapped me on the shoulder.

"Dad, who was *that*?"

"A man who knows his own importance," I said.

"His mother should have thrown *him* away and kept the *stork*," Vier said, and we both laughed.

Just then, Taitsie approached with Caroline Kennedy and her husband, Ed Schlossberg, in tow.

"Caroline and Ed," Taitsie said, "this is my soon-to-be-former husband, Theodore J. Higginbothem."

Vier shot his mother a disapproving glance and walked away. I could hear him mumbling under his breath, "She didn't have to say that...."

"Caroline and I are old friends from Newport," Taitsie told me. "She used to visit her mother's childhood home at Hammersmith Farm, and my father and Mummy would have her over at Bailey's Beach."

We shook hands. Caroline had a huge paw and her knuckles turned white as she gripped my hand. She wasn't someone you'd want to challenge to an arm wrestle.

"I thought you two should know each other," Taitsie said. "Higgy might not have been the world's greatest husband, but he's a first-rate literary agent. And, of course, Caroline writes books."

"I was just speaking with George Soros," I said, trying to make conversation. "That man's got all the warmth of a Frigidaire."

"People say, you know, the same, uh, about me, you know," Caroline said, and walked away.

To cover the embarrassing lapse, Taitsie asked, "Where are you staying?"

"In your guest room if that's okay with you."

Taitsie looked at me with a strange expression, but she didn't say anything.

A few minutes later, Vier and I gathered up our things and walked the two blocks to Taitsie's top-floor loft. It was the perfect apartment for an artist: one huge workspace crammed with sculpturing materials, buckets, stepladders, and even a hoisting device affixed to the ceiling. Taitsie had three bedrooms. Her master bedroom was at one end, next to a small kitchen. Vier's bedroom and the guest room were at the other end.

I reminded Vier that it was well past his bedtime.

"Oh, Dad, can't I stay up until Mom gets home so that we can all be together for a while?"

I shook my head. "Son, tomorrow's a school day. You and your mother and I'll have breakfast together in the morning before I leave."

He kissed me good night. He had the same strange expression that I had seen on Taitsie's face when I informed her that I was staying at her apartment.

I went to the guest room, unpacked, brushed my teeth in the adjoining bathroom, and went to bed. But I couldn't sleep. My mind kept replaying the events of the evening. George Soros' warning about how he was going to fix the economy and create a financial crisis so Barack Obama could win the White House... visions of the nude women portrayed in Taitsie's sculptures... the sight of Taitsie at the gallery....

Sometime after one o'clock in the morning, I awoke and found myself hungry. I realized I hadn't eaten anything since lunch. So I got up, threw on my trousers and a shirt and padded into the kitchen. Rummaging through the refrigerator, I saw a few items I could fashion into a sandwich. As I was spooning some mayonnaise onto a slice of health nut bread, a woman walked into the kitchen. She was dressed in a red teddy—the kind of sexy lingerie I used to buy for Taitsie. I stared in disbelief. It was one of the Desert Girls.

"Ah...hello," I stammered. "I'm Taitsie's husband."

I couldn't stop staring at her. She was even taller than she had appeared in the gallery. Her dark black hair cascaded over her shoulders and down her back. Her nipples showed through the red teddy. The woman was the most stunning creature I had ever seen.

Upon hearing that I was Taitsie's husband, she stiffened and took a small step back.

"I am Alem," she said in an accent that I immediately recognized as North African.

She didn't look happy at all.

"And I am Mihret," said the other Desert Girl as she came into the kitchen looking like a twin of the first.

The second Desert Girl was wearing a white towel wrapped around her torso. She looked as though she had just stepped out of the shower. What were these two beauties doing in Taitsie's kitchen, ready for bed, at one in the morning?

Before I could ask, I heard a voice coming from down the hall. It was Taitsie's voice.

My heart jumped.

"Girls, where are you?" she called.

The Desert Girls giggled and headed down the hall.

Curious, I couldn't help following them. I had to see the damning truth for myself. As I peered into the bedroom, I saw my wife sitting up in bed, wearing a filmy Oscar de la Renta nightgown.

I coughed to cover my confusion, then asked:

"Do you think we could try a little three-on-onesome?"

Taitsie's bellow to "Get *out!*" could have been heard all the way over in that strange, benighted land called New Jersey.

CHAPTER THIRTY-FIVE

At nine o'clock on a blustery weekday night, the wood-paneled bar at the Metropolitan Club, the most exclusive club in Washington, D.C., was deserted. The only other person in sight was the club's longtime bartender, Raul Famosa, a dapper Cuban American with one glass eye, who was closing up shop for the night.

"Good evening, Raul," I said.

"*Buenas tardes*, Señor Hijinbudun."

I had a warm spot in my heart for Raul. His father had worked undercover in Havana for the CIA before the Bay of Pigs invasion, and afterward The Deuce managed to get the whole family out of Cuba and bring them to the States. That was in 1962, when Raul was a fifteen-year-old punk with a thick Cuban accent. The Deuce straightened him out, made sure he got a high school diploma, and then arranged a job for him as a bartender at the Metropolitan Club.

In Raul's first days behind the bar, when I was still in my early twenties, I had inflicted some pretty serious collateral damage on his liquor inventory. I drank everything I could get my hands on: beer, bourbon, scotch, rum, and tequila. Oh, how I *loved* that tequila!

Then, after the club lifted its ban on women members in the late 1980s, Taitsie and I would enjoy drinking at the bar while we chatted with Raul, who passed along all the juiciest political gossip in Washington. Taitsie had introduced me to the subtle delights of sherry at the Metropolitan Club bar, as prelude to the more obvious pleasures of liquor-fueled *Sie müssen aufhören!*

A whole year had passed since that mortifying scene with the Desert Girls in Taitsie's bedroom. I had made several attempts to apologize for busting into their cozy trio. To no avail. She didn't want to have anything to do with me.

I sat down at the bar, and Raul Famosa pushed a paper coaster in my direction.

"Da jusual, Señor Hijinbudun. Club soda."

"Raul," I said, "screw the club soda. Give me a Hidalgo Manzanilla Pastrana sherry."

He arched an eyebrow over his glass eye, but didn't say a thing. He set a stemmed sherry glass on top of the paper coaster and filled it with pale gold liquid. I stared at the glass for a long moment, and then picked it up. My hand began to shake, and I spilled half the contents.

"Señor," Raul said, "ju gotta a problen or sometin' like dat?"

I drank the rest of the sherry in the glass

"Another!" I said.

He wiped the counter with a towel and poured me a second sherry.

"Leave the bottle," I said.

"Jais, Señor Hijinbudun."

"Raul, this country is going to hell," I said.

"So I unnerstan," he said

"Morality's out the window."

"Ju said it."

"I just got off the phone with my son," I said. "He told me something I've never heard before. Have you ever heard of a commitment ceremony among *three* people?"

"*Los trios!*" he said. "Dats how I got dis glass eye. From a *marido celoso.* A jay-lus hubund. A loon-*attic*! Caught me wid his wife."

"Pour me another."

"Jais, señor."

"This has nothing to do with a jealous *husband*," I said. "My boy tells me that his mother, who's been shacking up with not one but *two women*—that his mother wants to marry them *both!*"

Raul poured me a fourth sherry.

"Jur wife—I think chee has some 'splainin' to do."

My metabolic system wasn't used to alcohol, and my head was spinning.

"How can she commit to *two* women, for chrissakes?"

"In Cooba, we have a sayin'," Raul said. "*Mira que tiene cosa la mujer esta!* Whadda thing dis woman is!"

For a while, I sat there in silence, contemplating this nugget of wisdom, and Raul busied himself washing and drying glasses. Then, seeking an escape from my tortured thoughts, I looked over at Raul.

"Please turn on the TV."

"*Lo siento,* señor. Sorry. Club policy. No TV when da bar she's open."

"Fuck club policy!" I shouted. "Turn it on. Now!"

"*Si, señor.*"

He grabbed the remote and hit a button.

As usual, the TV was tuned to the Fox News Channel, and the screen filled with the face of Sean Hannity. The volume was on mute, so I couldn't hear what Hannity was saying. Only the facts chosen with the greatest discrimination, I was certain. Then, the screen cut to the Reverend Jeremiah A. Wright.

"Raul," I said, "turn on the volume!"

"Okai."

The Reverend Wright was standing at his church podium, dressed in a powder blue dashiki, and screaming at the top of his lungs.

> We have supported state terrorism against the Palestinians and black South Africans, and now we are indignant because the stuff we have done overseas is now brought right back to our own front

> yards. ...America's chickens are coming home to roost!

The scene on the television screen was chaotic. Congregants were rushing up to Reverend Wright and shaking his hand.

The Reverend Wright was all revved up.

> Racism is how this country was founded and how this country is still run!... We in the U.S. believe in white supremacy and black inferiority and believe it more than we believe in God.

Sean Hannity was back on the screen.

"Senator Obama's friend, the Reverend Wright, is saying these things," Hannity said, shaking his head. "We have to ask: How is this going to affect his campaign?"

I knew damn well how this was going to affect Barack Obama's campaign. If I wasn't too drunk to think straight—and I felt instantly sobered by what I had just seen—the anti-white, anti-American tirade by the Reverend Jeremiah Wright could write finis to Obama's presidential aspirations.

Barack Obama had some 'splainin' to do.

CHAPTER THIRTY-SIX

Late the next afternoon, I assembled the members of the Tchaikovsky Circle in the conference room of MITT, the Midwestern Institute for Traditional Thinking.

"Folks," I began, "we've been handed a golden opportunity. These Reverend Wright video recordings with their attacks on the United States have created a firestorm. Obama's been a member of that church for twenty years. How can he wriggle out of *this* one? Those video recordings have the potential to turn the presidential campaign on its head."

"Higgy," Russ Slanover said, "the Trinity United Church has a website called www.g-damnAmerica.com. They're selling DVDs of the Reverend Wright's sermons."

"Oh great," I said. "I just can't wait to get the Reverend Wright's Greatest Hits Album with all-time faves like 'Jews Done Bitch-Slapped Us,' 'Lying Honky Motherfuckah', and—"

"One Sunday," said Vangie Roll, interrupting me, "the Reverend Wright showed Mom and me all his videotaping and editing equipment down in the vestry basement."

"If we can *prove* that Obama sat there in a church pew while the Reverend was spouting off at the mouth..." Russ Slanover said.

"I'll go Russ one better," Vangie said. "Mom heard from a neighbor—a longtime congregant at Trinity United—who was there one Sunday morning about two years ago when the Reverend really went off like a rocket and said that the American government owed every black man, woman and child $100,000 in reparations—*per year.*

"And," Vangie continued, "Mom says that this neighbor swore to her that Barack Obama was sitting in his usual seat in the front pew when the Reverend Wright made this statement. He personally saw Barack Obama stand up, walk to the podium, and high-five the Reverend Wright."

"Jesus!" said Sydney Michael Green. "Do they have *that* on tape?"

No one said a word for a moment.

"Folks," I said, slapping the conference table for emphasis, "we have to assume that every minute of every church service has been recorded, and that a DVD of Obama high-fiving the Reverend Wright after that sermon is somewhere down in the basement of the church vestry office."

"*Some*where," said Sydney Michael Green. "But *where*?"

"And," added Russ Slanover, "who can we send down there to get it?"

"I think I know the *perfect* person," I said.

CHAPTER THIRTY-SEVEN

Less than a week later, I found myself wedged into the back of a van along with Russ Slanover and a ton of high-tech surveillance equipment. The van was parked one hundred yards from the entrance of the Trinity United Church, and Russ was doing a last-minute check of the TV and audio signals coming from the Tchaikovsky Circle's secret operative, who was, at this very moment, descending in a church elevator on her way to the basement.

"Can you hear me now?"

It was the breathless voice of Elvira Roll speaking to us wirelessly from inside the elevator.

"You're coming through loud and clear, Elvira," I said.

Over the objections of Vangie Roll, I had dispatched her mother on this dangerous clandestine mission. Despite her age and advanced emphysema, Elvira was the natural candidate to steal the incriminating video recordings of Barack Obama congratulating the Reverend Wright on his anti-American rant. Because of her warm relationship with the Reverend Wright, Elvira's presence in the vestry basement wouldn't raise any suspicions. And she knew exactly where the video recordings were stored—in an unlocked cabinet next to the handicapped restroom.

What's more, Elvira was eager to go. As she put it: "I didn't work my ass off with Thurgood Marshall on *Brown* v. *Board of Education* and a dozen other Supreme Court civil-rights cases just to see some cheap and worthless clown undo all the advancement blacks have made in this country. Unlike some others, I am *always* proud of my country."

Russ Slanover nudged me with an elbow and pointed to the TV screen. We could see the elevator doors open.

"How about now?" Elvira said into the microphone that was embedded in the headrest of her motorized wheelchair. "Can you hear me now?"

"Elvira," I said, exasperated, "this isn't a Verizon commercial. You don't have to keep asking if I can hear you now. Your equipment is state-of-the-art National Security Agency hardware, and it's working perfectly. Russ and I can hear and see everything that you can hear and see. We can even hear your lungs wheezing."

As the mechanized wheelchair left the elevator, the miniature TV camera adapted to the change in light and transmitted a picture from about two feet above the floor. Elvira turned left along a long corridor and approached several people—or several sets of legs and feet. The electronically controlled camera adjusted silently until it moved in on the faces in front of Elvira.

The faces belonged to a bevy of the Reverend Wright's attractive young female assistants.

Elvira continued to cruise down the hallway. We heard the voice of a woman say, "Good morning, Elvira. Good to see you."

"Good morning to you, too, dear," Elvira replied.

Up ahead, the hallway split into a T, and Elvira made a right-hand turn. She passed the conference room where, four years earlier, I had attended the Reverend Wright's organizational Obama-for-president meeting. Elvira continued on at a rapid clip until she reached the handicapped restroom.

Russ and I could hear new voices in the distance. As Elvira moved closer to the source of the sounds, I recognized the voice of the Reverend Wright.

"Now...watch *this* video! It's a real beaut!"

Elvira inched nearer, and I heard the Reverend Wright's recorded voice.

"*No, no, no!*" he screamed. "Not God *bless* America—God*damn* America! That's in the Bible for killing innocent people. God*damn* America for treating our citizens as less than human. God*damn* America for as long as she acts like she is God and she is supreme...."

Then, all at once, I heard a different man's voice.

"Goddamn America," said this man. "Now *that* is indeed a sentiment I can drink to!"

The hidden camera picked up the figure of a woman approaching Elvira. I recognized her as the Reverend Wright's personal secretary.

"Oh, it's *you*, Elvira. The pastor was hoping you would drop by. He'd love for you to come into his office and meet a new visitor to Trinity United. They've been viewing video clips of some of the Reverend's old sermons."

"I'd be happy to," Elvira said.

As she rolled into the Reverend's large, well-appointed office, Russ and I could see a male visitor sitting in one of the comfortable armchairs across from the Reverend's desk. His back was to the camera.

"What's *that*?" Russ said, pointing to something on the floor next to this visitor's feet.

"It looks like a dog," I said.

We could see the Reverend Wright get out of his chair and come over to greet Elvira. He bent over and gave her a peck on the cheek.

"Good morning, my lady! I'm surely glad you dropped by. I want you to meet a new friend of Trinity United."

Just then the dog sprang to its feet and looked straight into the wheelchair camera. Then, from behind the dog, a *second* dog appeared, identical to the first. Neither was leashed. They both came toward Elvira and began to smell her.

Elvira's wheezing grew worse.

"*Saditius*!" the visitor commanded his dogs.

I recognized the Russian command for "*Sit!*" I started to get an uneasy feeling.

Both dogs immediately sat down.

"This is my number one congregant," the Reverend said, introducing Elvira Roll. "She represents CLIT, the Chicago Low Income Trust."

The man shook hands with Elvira.

"I am Yurik Maligin," he said. "And these are my Russian wolfhounds— Molotov and Cocktail."

"Elvira," the Reverend said, "Mr. Maligin just made a most generous contribution to our church."

Elvira grunted.

"I don't believe this," Russ Slanover whispered into my ear. "Maligin is donating money to the Reverend Wright?"

"And you can bet that the price for that donation was the Obama high-five DVD," I said.

"You're right, Higgy," Russ said. "Look—Maligin is carrying a box of DVDs."

"Reverend," Maligin said, preparing to depart. "It's been a great pleasure to meet you. I commend you and your ministry. I will now leave you and Miss Roll to your business."

With that, he barked another one-word command—"*Piata!*"—and Molotov and Cocktail heeled on each side of Maligin as he exited the room.

The Reverend Wright sat down and faced Elvira. He had a big grin on his face. He held up a check and showed it to Elvira. The hidden camera zoomed in and picked up the image: it was a Bank of Monaco cashier's check made out to "Trinity United/ Reverend J.A. Wright Jr. Private Account."

I stared in stunned disbelief at the astronomical figure on the check: a cool half a million dollars.

Before I had a chance to recover from the shock, there was a sudden loud knock at the door of our van. I stood up and pushed open the door. Standing there was Yurik Maligin, flanked by his two Russian wolfhounds.

"Comrade Higgy!" he said, looking up at me with a mock smile. "Excuse me for interrupting your pathetic surveillance operation. But you may recall that many, many years ago, back in London, I promised that I'd outfox you. Well, that day has come. I *have* outfoxed you. I've got it *all*. I've got Mombasa and Honolulu and the real truth about Barack Obama's birth. I've got Indonesia and the foreskin. And now, to cap it all off, I've got the tapes from Trinity United.

"Comrade Higgy," he went on, "pardon me if I savor the moment of my greatest triumph. But now we must face facts. *I've* got the Obama file and *you* don't! And as my favorite American comedian, Jackie Gleason, used to say, 'How sweet it is!' "

CHAPTER THIRTY-EIGHT

On a cool November election night, I made my way to Chicago's Grant Park to witness Barack Obama's victory rally. I felt unhinged and demented. Why had I come to Grant Park? Was it a masochistic streak in my personality that carried me here to join a throng of more than one hundred thousand delirious people celebrating the triumph of The Chosen One?

The jumbotron showed the soon-to-be First Family sitting in the holding room. I also recognized David Axelrod talking to Imam Selatin, Barack Obama's Muslim teacher, and Grandma Bibi Obama and Malik Obama, Barack's half brother. Grandma Bibi was decked out in a diamond necklace with matching earrings and bracelets. Her gold teeth had diamonds encrusted in them, too. I wonder who paid for all of that ice?

I soon found the answer to my own question when the jumbotron zoomed in on an odd-looking couple: a short man with a strikingly beautiful young blonde woman carrying a Chinese Crested hairless accessory dog. Countess Gladys of Thurn und

Taxis was accompanied by Yurik Maligin. He had a huge shit-eating grin on his face.

Next, the jumbotron scanned the crowd, settling on a group of women in front of a large sign: MARRIAGE FOR ALL WHO WANT IT

"Let's ask one of these women what the election of Barack Obama means for them?" said the TV reporter.

"Tonight means my two girlfriends and I can legally have a civil union and get married. The three of us are ecstatic. We love Obama!"

It was Taitsie—with a triumphant smile on her face—and the Desert Girls. The three of them had their arms wrapped around each other. My stomach turned.

Suddenly, a hand came out of nowhere and grabbed my shoulder. I turned to see George Soros, the billionaire currency speculator.

"Good to run into you tonight," he said. "I told you I'd arrange for things to work out *my* way! Just like I predicted, I created the greatest financial collapse since the Great Depression in order to make sure that George W. Bush would get the blame and Obama would be the champion of hope and change...."

In the middle of this swaggering speech, Obama and his family appeared on the stage, and the crowd began chanting, "Yes we can!... Yes we can!... Yes we can!"

Whatever it was that had brought me to Grant Park, those three words convinced me that the tide of history had turned decisively against the CIA. The American people had chosen a new messiah – and this man was *not* the messiah that the CIA would have chosen for them.

"Yes we can!" the crowd continued to roar. *"Yes we can!"*

No I can't, I thought. *No I can't.*

CHAPTER THIRTY-NINE

After I arrived back at my hotel suite, I zipped open the leather Louis Vuitton Dopp kit that Taitsie had given me for my thirty-seventh birthday and removed several bottles of Vicodan and Percocet. Each time I refilled the prescriptions for back pain, I had made sure to put aside half of the pills for just this moment.

The idea of taking my own life had been rattling around in my brain for the past four years. I had found a book at a used bookstore off Dupont Circle entitled *How to Guarantee a Successful Suicide and Other Useful Tips for Improving Your Life.* And I had placed a call to the office of Dr. Jack Kevorkian to schedule a consultation. But the voice on the other end of the phone answered, "Lucinda's House of Nails. This is Lucinda, known as Lucky, which you will be if you schedule an appointment." When I asked for Dr. Kevorkian, she told me, "Honey, the doc's in the can…and I don't mean the shitter."

I took off my jacket and tie and shoes, and called down to room service and ordered a bottle of Hidalgo Manzanilla Pastrana sherry.

"I'm sorry, Mr. Higginbothem," the operator said, "but we don't carry that brand of sherry."

I couldn't imagine committing suicide without my favorite brand of sherry.

"Okay," I said, "then send someone out to get a bottle."

"It's after two in the morning, Mr. Higginbothem. There aren't any liquor stores open."

"Then call around to other hotels," I said. "One of them must carry Hidalgo Manzanilla Pastrana sherry. *Just get it!*"

I sat down at the desk, and removed several pages of Ambassador East Hotel stationery from the drawer. I unscrewed the cap on my Graf von Faber-Castel pen, which was made of Indian satinwood and had been voted 2008 Pen of the Year.

I began to write a farewell note to my Dad when a knock on the door interrupted my concentration.

"Yes?" I called out.

"Room service" came the reply.

I opened the door and a waiter brought in a small silver tray with a bottle of Hidalgo Manzanilla Pastrana sherry.

"Great!" I said. "You found it!"

"We were able to track down the sherry you requested from the Hotel Burnham," he said. "Only, I must tell you, sir, that the contents are more than half gone."

"Well, it's a start," I said. "Tell the manager at the desk I need another bottle—a full one. And pronto!"

I handed him a big tip, and he was gone.

I left the door unlocked in anticipation of his return. At the writing desk, I felt a stabbing pain in the lower left side of my back. I poured two piles of pills into the palm of my hand—one of Vicodan and one of Percocet—then shoved them all into my mouth. I washed them down with the sherry.

I tried to stand up. But for a moment I couldn't move! I fell to my knees and screamed out, "God, please make it stop! Please!"

And suddenly the pain *did* stop.

A wonderful, warm, comforting feeling invaded my body. And I saw this scene, not through my own eyes, but from above. I had somehow left my body and floated to the ceiling of the hotel room.

I saw a man who I knew was Jesus Christ. I was certain of it. He stood in front of me and wrapped His arms around me. Suddenly I felt better than I have ever felt in my life. I was at total peace.

And Jesus spoke to me.

"The-o-*dore*," he said, "you really look like a wreck."

CHAPTER FORTY

I heard voices coming from the black void of space.

"Doctor, how's my husband?"

"We've pumped his stomach, Mrs. Higginbothem...."

"Will he live?"

"The hospital's procedure is to continue to list him as serious until we get his vital signs stabilized...."

The female voice came much closer. "Bottom, oh my dear, dear *Bottom*, why did you do this to yourself? *Why?*"

"You've *got* to go now, Mrs. Higginbothem."

"Oh, Bottom, my love, can you hear me?"

"Ma'am, *please*! We need to move your husband into radiology for the insertion of the percutaneous nephrostomy tube..."

"Doctor, tell him I was here. Tell him Taitsie was here...."

"Who?"

"His wife. *Taitsie*."

"You've got to be kidding...."

My brain was so clouded by the effects of the overdose of prescription narcotics that I couldn't process smatterings of conversation. I heaved in and out of consciousness, and not until several hours later did I begin to make some sense of what had happened to me.

A tiny Filipina nurse by the name of Girlie informed me that I was in Mercy Hospital and Medical Center on South Michigan Avenue in downtown Chicago. An Ambassador East room service waiter, who was bringing me a fresh, unopened bottle of Hidalgo Manzanilla Pastrana sherry, had found me unconscious and sprawled on the floor of my hotel room. Jesus was right: it wasn't a very dignified way to die. The hotel acted swiftly and summoned an ambulance, which had brought me here to the ER.

"When they pumped your stomach," Girlie said, "they ran all sorts of tests and they found a huge kidney stone at the top of your urethra, which had been causing your back pain. The doctors are amazed you were walking around with a stone that large for so long." Such a medical marvel had her in a state of rhapsody. "Now you know what childbirth feels like. The doctors anesthetized you and inserted a tube right into your kidney—ugh!— area and removed the stone."

"Forget the stone," I said. "How did the hospital find my wife?"

"The organ donor card in your wallet had your wife's name listed as next of kin," Girlie explained. "We reached her on her cell phone, and she rushed right over here. You're a lucky man to have a wife like that, Mr. Higginbothem."

Lucky? A wife that would turn down a chance at a three-on-onesome?

Then I caught myself and wondered: Why had Taitsie come to the hospital? What did Taitsie's visit mean? Did she still have feelings for me? Was there any hope whatsoever that I could win her back?

In the middle of my gaudy musings, the phone next to my hospital bed started ringing.

"It's your son," Girlie said, handing me the receiver.

"Hey, Dad, how're you doing?" Vier said. "Mom told me you almost died...from food poisoning. I hope you're better now."

"I'm coming along just great," I said, relieved that Taitsie had not told Vier the truth about my attempted suicide. "Nothing to worry about, son."

"Dad, can I come and see you? Being the only man in a house of women who blabber nonstop is getting seriously old."

CHAPTER FORTY-ONE

Several weeks later, pain-free and sober, I was staring out of a big bay window at Heron Point, a secret CIA campus just outside Chestertown, on Maryland's Eastern Shore. Tucked away in a corner of this wooded compound was a small rehab clinic for CIA personnel who had run into drug and drinking problems. The program was called S.A.D.D.—Substance Abuse, Drug and Depression—and successful graduates were referred to around the CIA as SADD-Sacks.

After a knock on the door, my supervising counselor at Heron Point, who went by the moniker McQ, entered the room. He had a nose the size of a doorknob and a face with a million broken veins.

"Hey, man," McQ said, "can I come in?

"As Whitney Nutwing would say, *La mia casa è la tua casa.*"

"That sounds just like Nutwing," McQ said. "So, how ya doing, man?"

"How do I look?"

"Like a new man, man," he said. "I'm really impressed by your recovery. You're trim, you're fit—"

"And," I interrupted him, "eager to begin life again. I want to go home and see my son. I miss him terribly. And as for Taitsie, I'm determined to win her back and fill the emptiness I've felt since the day she left me."

"I'm glad you've been able to talk in the AA rooms about your feelings for Taitsie," McQ said. "That's healthy, man. And I was really impressed by your dream of creating a 'Girls of the CIA' wall calendar and making Valerie Plame the month of January. But don't forget, when you see Taitsie, remember it's *you* who's supposed to make amends. Not the other way around. Got it?"

"I got it."

"By the way, you've got visitors waiting outside. Whitney Nutwing and The Deuce. Can they come in?"

"Sure, bring them in."

I hadn't seen either man since the Ambassador East incident. In fact, I hadn't seen anyone from my past. But during all this time I had never felt alone or abandoned. As a born-again Christian, I had the rocklike support of my new best friend and Higher Power, Jesus Christ, who had shone me the light on election night, and was now with me each and every day. I started thinking, those portraits had him all wrong. Someone as enlightened as that wouldn't have dressed in dirty robes. He would have had a sense of style. He would have ditched that beard. He would have walked around wearing—

Nutwing and The Deuce came into the room, bearing flowers and broad smiles.

"The-o-*dore*...you look ten years younger!" Nutwing exclaimed.

"Can't say the same for you," I said after he released me from his moist, warm grip. "Looks like you put on some more weight."

"A pound or two, Higgy. A pound or two. But then, who's counting?"

The Deuce and I exchanged a manly father-son handshake.

"Throw on a warm jacket and let's go outside," The Deuce said. "Mr. Nutwing and I have something we want to discuss with you."

Nutwing led the way to a heated golf cart that was waiting at the front door. He and The Deuce sat in the front; I climbed into the back. Nutwing hit the accelerator, and we sped off to a part of the campus that was usually off-limits to SADD-Sacks like me.

As we drove through the woods, we passed a shooting range and heard the muffled pistol fire of target practice. We also passed a wooden building designated CLOSE-COMBAT/HAND-TO-HAND, where years before a CIA-trainee by the name of Tina Fey had accidentally received her facial scar.

Nutwing drove us to a secluded corner of Heron Point, which was segregated from the rest of the campus by a high barbed-wire fence. A heavily armed security team manning the gate waved us through.

Nutwing stopped the golf cart in front of a wooden building marked ENHANCED INTERROGATION TRAINING CENTER.

"I hope you didn't bring me here to interrogate me," I said, half-joking. "I'll confess to anything. I'm a T.F.F.—a Total Fucking Failure."

"Not in *my* eyes, you're not," The Deuce said. "Higgy, I've always been proud of you, and I'm proud of you right now. McQ's told me all about your remarkable recovery. Personally, I wouldn't want to see Valerie Plame on that CIA calendar you have in mind, but that's only a quibble. All in all, if I could choose a son all over again, I'd choose you."

"Thanks, Dad," I said, deeply touched.

"And The-o-*dore*," Nutwing added, "we're not here to talk about the *past*. We're here to discuss your *future* assignment. As you know, Barack Obama is going to be inaugurated next week. Whether we like it or not, Obama's the only president we've got. So, it's time to reassess our approach—*drop* our investigation of Obama and *start* doing everything in our power to *protect* him. That's going to be a tall order. From what I've seen in your confidential Obama work-up, Yurik Maligin has collected damaging goods on Obama. And, no doubt, the Russians are prepared to use this information to put the squeeze on our new president."

"Yes," I said, "the Russians will use the incriminating information that Maligin has collected on Obama to blackmail him...try to make him cancel America's plans for an anti-ballistic-missile system in Poland and Czechoslovakia...try to make him back off NATO membership for Ukraine...try to make him replace the Statue of Liberty with a large-scale set of Russian *matryoshka* nesting dolls...."

"That's exactly what I was afraid of," Nutwing said dryly. "So here's your new mission. We want you to meet personally with President Obama."

"Meet? With Obama?"

"Yes, you and Barack are about to become great friends."

CHAPTER FORTY-TWO

I heard screaming sirens and saw a Secret Service motorcade with motorcycle outriders, black SUV's, an ambulance, and two long, dark limousines. The motorcade streamed through the gates and pulled to a stop. Half a dozen Secret Service agents hopped out and surrounded one of the limos. They had those transparent wires running from their sleeves up their necks to their ears. On a silent command, they opened the back right door.

Out stepped Dick Cheney, the soon-to-be ex vice president of the United States, looking grim and sour. He strode toward the wooden ENHANCED INTERROGATION TRAINING CENTER building. Following in his tracks were a blonde woman and several male staffers.

Nutwing, The Deuce and I climbed out of the golf cart and followed Cheney into the building. It had been turned into a mockup of a Middle Eastern prison. It was dark and dusty, and the smell reminded me of an Arab souk. A CIA man addressed Cheney.

"Sir, when you're ready, change into a standard-issue detainee orange jumpsuit. Then come back out here."

Cheney nodded, took a folded set of clothing from a staffer, and headed into changing room. A couple of minutes later, he emerged looking like a Gitmo prisoner of war.

The CIA guys running the operation grabbed Cheney and shackled his hands together. Then they chained his feet so he could only shuffle along. Two members of his Secret Service detail leaped forward to protect the soon-to-be ex v.p.

"Stand back!" Cheney barked at his Secret Service bodyguards. "It's all right. Let's do this!"

The CIA men dragged Cheney over to a low metal table and forced him to lie on it, face up, with his head hanging over the edge. They strapped him tight. Suddenly, the blonde woman who had followed him into the building started shouting.

"Daddy!" cried Liz Cheney, his conservative firebrand daughter, "I'm worried all that water's going to short-circuit your pacemaker."

But the CIA agents didn't pay any attention to her. They produced a dirty-looking rag and a bucket of water. They spread the rag over Dick Cheney's face and slowly pored the water over the rag.

Cheney began squirming like a fish thrown on the deck of a boat. But the two CIA men held him down as they screamed at him.

"Tell us about your ties to Al Qaeda… When is the next attack… We can do this all day if you want… We're going to wipe your ass with the Koran…."

This went on for several minutes, and I thought they were going to kill the old guy. Then, without warning, the CIA men stopped the interrogation. They unshackled Cheney and stood him up. He was gasping for breath. He looked like a beaten man. His white hair was frazzled and his orange jumpsuit was wet down to his waist. But, for the first time since his arrival, a huge smile came over his wide mouth.

"I *loved* that!" he said. "I *loved* getting water boarded! Can we do it again? Come on, fellas. Water board me again! *Please*!"

Whitney Nutwing pulled me aside and pressed something into my hand.

I looked down and saw that it was my suicide note.

Nutwing smiled and nodded toward The Deuce, who was walking out of the building.

"After your botched suicide, we swept your hotel room," Nutwing said. "The Deuce never saw your suicide note."

"Thanks," I whispered.

"You owe me big time," Nutwing said. "So here's your new mission. I want you to go the White House on Inauguration Day, introduce yourself to President Obama and inform him that the CIA has designated you as his John the Baptist."

"His *what*?"

"John the *Baptist*," Nutwing repeated. "As a born-again Christian, you must know who John the Baptist is. You're going to prepare the way and purify the waters for Barack Obama—The Chosen One, the Messiah, the Deliverer of our nation! You're going to protect President Obama from the Russians—and from his own worst instincts. You're going to be his John the Baptist."

"If I remember my Bible accurately," I said, "wasn't John the Baptist the guy who was beheaded?"

BOOK THREE

CHAPTER FORTY-THREE

After his inauguration at the Capitol, Barack Obama motorcaded to the Oval Office, where Sydney Michael Green and I were waiting for him along with his White House Secret Service detail, his secretarial staff, and his three closest aides— Valerie Jarrett, Rahm Emanuel and David Axelrod. Needless to say, I didn't invite Sydney Michael Green. He was there courtesy of Whitney Nutwing, who ordered him to keep an eye on me.

Everyone in the room broke into applause as the 44th president of the United States strode into the Oval. He took his place behind the Resolute Desk, a large, nineteenth-century partner's desk that was a gift from Queen Victoria to President Rutherford B. Hayes in 1880 and was built from the timbers of the Arctic exploration ship H.M.S. *Resolute*.

"Let it be recorded that these were my first words as president," Obama declared. "I. Am. Where. I. Was. Always. *Destined*. To. Be."

"Sock it to 'em, baby!" Sydney Michael Green blurted out.

Obama ignored the outburst and leaned back and threw his long legs up on the Resolute Desk. In an instant a Filipino steward rushed forward carrying a portable basin and a bucket of water. The steward began unlacing the president's shoes.

"What's going on?" Obama asked, starting to pull away. "I only take my shoes off in a mosque."

"Relax and enjoy it," said Rahm Emanuel.

The steward removed Obama's shoes and socks and began washing his feet.

"Mmm…that feels *soooo* good," Obama said, wiggling his toes.

"Get used to it," said Emanuel. "My first order as your chief of staff was to give your steward, Disaderio, instructions to come in here twice a day and wash your feet."

"That reminds me of the old Bob Marley lyrics," said Valerie Jarrett. She broke into song and started dancing the reggae around the Resolute Desk:

Who are you to judge the life I live?
I know I'm not perfect —

"Not perfect?" Obama shouted. He stood bolt upright and, in the process, spilled the entire basin of soapy water over the Resolute Desk.

"Of *course* you're perfect," said David Axelrod, mopping up the water with his necktie. "You're unrivaled, unequal, matchless, incomparable, peerless, unsurpassed—"

"You're the top," said Rahm Emanuel. "You're the Coliseum."

"You're tutti frutie," said Valerie Jarrett.

"A-wop-bop-a-loo-bop-a-lop-bop-bop!" said Sydney Michael Green.

"Sir," I said, trying to wedge my way into this songfest, "I'm your John the Baptist from the CIA."

"Welcome, John," Obama said. "Nice to have you onboard."

"Call me Higgy," I said.

"Folks, meet John. Hey, wait a second. Haven't we met before, John?"

"Yes, sir, in fact we have," I said. "Several years ago, I came to see you at the *Harvard Law Review* about becoming your literary agent."

"Oh, yeah," Obama said. "I remember that day. I told you back then that I'd write a bestseller and it'd catapult me to national stardom and that I'd become the first African-American president. I was right, wasn't I?" I could tell he really liked the idea of being right. "How was I dressed that day? In my Gold Trumpeter suit, I'll bet. Was my hair longer then? Did I look lean? I was into high-impact aerobics back then. Hadn't begun golf. Shot an 83 the other day. My putting needs work..."

Sydney Michael Green leaned toward me and whispered, "I counted ten 'I's' and four 'me's.' "

"You missed three 'my's,'" I replied sharply.

Valerie Jarrett approached the president. "Barry...uh... Mr. President," she said, "the wardrobe mirrors that you ordered have been installed on the back of every door here in the Oval Office. That way, when you're alone, you will be with your favorite person."

"Sir," I continued, "As your John the Baptist, I'm here to brief you on highly classified matters."

"I want a smoke," the President said petulantly.

Sydney Michael Green produced a Marlboro and a gold lighter with the presidential seal on it.

"Don't tell Michelle," Obama said, taking a deep drag on the cigarette.

"Don't worry, I won't," Sydney Michael Green said.

Obama looked at him with a weird expression that said "who is this guy?"

Rahm Emanuel snapped his fingers and three short, barely dressed Thai boys appeared carrying large palm-leaf fans. They deployed themselves around President Obama, who was already engulfed in a cloud of cigarette smoke. The boys kneeled on the floor and began fanning the smoke toward an open Oval Office window.

"Mr. President," I continued, "it is my responsibility to alert you about any potentially dangerous security problems. We at the CIA have it on good authority that Moscow has an extensive file on you, Mr. President. A file loaded with blackmail material ranging from the truth about your birth right up through your days in Chicago. The Russians' top operative, Yurik Maligin, intends to force you to withdraw the anti-missile systems from Eastern Europe and to decrease American influence in the Middle East."

"Hey, you never know," Sydney Michael Green butted in. "Those Russians might force you to approve the construction of a mosque at Ground Zero."

President Obama waved Sydney Michael Green away and walked over to one of the floor-to-ceiling mirrors and peered at himself. Then he turned to me and said, "Do you dance, John?"

"Do I *what*?" I said.

"Dance," he said. "You must know the basics of ballroom dancing."

"Yes, sir," I said. "I do."

"Good," the president said. "Your first assignment is to stand in for Michelle as I rehearse for my Inaugural Balls tonight. Here we go."

The president signaled Valerie Jarrett, who played a slow fox trot on her iPod. Obama raised his left hand and grabbed my right hand in it. He cupped his right hand around the middle of my spine and began leading me around the newly installed Oval Office rug, which was embossed with his chin-up profile.

"Slow…slow…quick, quick, quick…slow…that's the rhythm, John… You're not a bad dancer."

"Call me Higgy, Mr. President."

For the next five minutes, we danced around the two sofas and two armchairs, with the president of the United States repeatedly studying his image in the mirrors.

When he was satisfied with his dancing, he said, "Okay, that's enough."

A staffer ran over and blotted his sweaty brow with a tissue.

"John, here's the first thing I want you to do," the president said. "I want you to make sure I get the Olympics in 2016 for Chicago. I have plans to rename Chicago after me. *Obama, Illinois*. Sounds good, doesn't it? After that, we're going to make Obama, Illinois, the new capital of the United States. I mean, after all, why should a slave owner like George Washington be the namesake of the nation's capital?"

Just then one of the mirrored doors opened and Vice President Joe Biden stumbled in. He caught his reflection in the mirror, twirled around, and began working on his hair and practicing his smile.

"After you get the 2016 Olympics, John," the president continued, ignoring his vice president, "I want you to find a way to pass my energy bill—cap-and-trade."

"Who's this Captain Trade? " Joe Biden asked.

"Sir," said one of the staffers, "it's cap *and* trade."

"I know," Biden said. "But why does the Senate have a bill named after *him*?"

"Sir," the staffer tried again, "it's a bill to set up a system to reward conservation of energy. And it creates a way to trade clean energy credits."

"Well," said Biden, "you can count on this proud son of Delaware from the steel mills of Pennsylvania as being in favor of anything that's clean. With the exception, of course, of energy."

No one dared to contradict the vice president.

Meanwhile, the president continued with his list of demands.

"On the campuses," he said, "I want the textbooks completely rewritten. They need to explain how every problem we have in this country is the Republicans' fault and that I came along to save the country. You shouldn't have too much trouble getting those lefty professors to write *that*, eh?

"Finally, John, there's the issue of my life *after* the presidency," he continued. "Of course there'll be the books and speeches and the presidential library…and I'll make millions… But I'm already so big that that won't suffice. So here's what I want you to do for me, John. I want you to make a plan to put my likeness up on Mount Rushmore. And that, for the moment, is all I can think of. You can go."

He dismissed me with a wave of his cigarette.

As I turned to leave the Oval, David Axelrod called after me.

"Hey, John," he said, "don't get the wrong impression. These mirrors aren't here just to boost the president's ego. They're here as a symbolic statement that the Oval is only a reflection of the *real* government. If you want to know how the Obama administration is really going to work, go down to the Situation Room."

"Thanks for the tip," I said.

"Any time, John," Axelrod said, wringing the water out of his necktie.

"Call me Higgy."

CHAPTER FORTY-FOUR

At David Axelrod's suggestion, I made my way down to the Situation Room, the mammoth, five thousand-square-foot conference area and intelligence-management center in the basement of the White House. This was where the president, in times of crisis, exercised control, influence, and authority—The Deuce's triad of power.

The first person I ran into was the Reverend Jeremiah Wright. He was using his iPhone to take snapshots of Bill Ayers, who was sitting at the head of the long wooden table in the president's chair.

"Man," said Ayers, fingering the buttons and communication equipment, "can you just picture the bombings I could orchestrate from here! *Pow!* There goes the Pentagon. *Pow!* There goes the State Department.... *Pow!* There goes the Palm restaurant..."

The Reverend Wright looked up from his iPhone and noticed me.

"Alfie Douglas!" he said, surprise written all over his face. "What are *you* doin' here?"

"Uh, hello, pastor," I said, trying to think of a convincing explanation for my presence. "The Chicago Low Income Trust asked me to scout locations for our CLIT convention next month. We're thinking of renting the Situation Room and inviting the rapper Eminem to sing for us."

"Don't say?" the Reverend Wright said. I detected a tone of suspicion in his voice. "Tell me, what song is that white honky rapper goin' to sing anyways?"

"*The Real Slim Shady*," I said.

"Never heard of it," he said. "Sounds *shady* to me. Let me hear *you* sing it…if you can?"

I had no choice. I was on the spot. So I began to sing:

"Slim Shady, I'm sick of him
Look at him, walkin around grabbin his you-know-what—

"Gentlemen," one of the Situation Room duty officers said, mercifully interrupting my off-key singing, "the Joint Chiefs of Staff are going to need this room in less than an hour to discuss a crisis in Afghanistan, and so I think you should get started with the people you asked to interview."

"Bring 'em on, bring 'em on!" the Reverend Wright said.

Four men entered the room and took seats around the table. "We're here tonight to put in place the *real* Administration, not the one upstairs, which operates with cigarette smoke and mirrors," said the Reverend Wright. "You folks are going to be sent out to various departments to keep an eye on people. You're going to enforce our *real* policies."

The heads of the four men nodded in unison.

"And we're going to call you czars. Like in the old days in Russia. You're going to boss people around and pay no attention to their opinions."

As I listened, the Reverend Wright's words triggered a memory of my childhood in Isfahan, the ancient capital of Iran. I recalled the fateful day that the Deuce had taken me aside and lectured me on his great-man philosophy of politics. How had the Deuce put it?

"Democracy gives the poor, weak, pathetic mob the illusion that they have power and that they're running things. Whereas in fact the mob has to be ruled by strong and powerful men."

Bill Ayers cleared his throat and broke my reverie.

"What the Reverend Wright is saying is that there are really *two* governments," Ayers said. "The public one that we see on TV. White bread. Boring. Safe. Mainstream. And then there's the *real* Obama government. Radical. *Revolutionary!* Out to make fundamental changes from top to bottom."

So far, there hadn't been a peep from the four men at the table.

The Reverend Wright opened a file.

"Now you, Dr. Holdren," the Reverend said, pointing to a man with a bushy Van Dyck beard. "We have you penciled in for Science and Technology Czar. Back in the late

1970s, you co-authored a textbook in which you offered ideas for coercive, involuntary fertility control, including—and I quote—'a program of sterilizing women after their second or third child.' You also discussed in that book the development of an 'armed international organization, a global analogue of a police force' to which nations would surrender part of their sovereignty.

"Are those your true words, Dr. Holdren, and do you still stand by them?" the Reverend Wright asked.

"My *exact* words, from my textbook *Ecoscience*, are these," Dr. John Holdren said. He read from a book open in front of him.

> Indeed, it has been concluded that compulsory population-control laws, even including laws requiring compulsory abortion, could be sustained under the existing Constitution if the population crisis became sufficiently severe to endanger society.

"And what about single mothers having their babies taken away by the government?" the Reverend Wright asked.

"I wrote," Dr. Holdren said, "that one way to carry out this disapproval of out-of-wedlock births might be to insist that all illegitimate babies be put up for adoption."

"Consider yourself President Obama's Science Czar," Bill Ayers said. "Bravo!"

The Reverend Wright turned to the next man.

"Professor Cass Sunstein," he said, "we particularly liked your legal paper arguing that animals should have the right to bring lawsuits against their owners. So, we're moving you over to be our Regulatory Czar. You're going to oversee *all* our new regulations. And there's going to be a lot of them, let me tell you...."

While the Reverend Wright was talking to Professor Sunstein, I studied the third man at the table— a sturdy-looking fellow with a shaved head. He looked familiar. Then I realized that I knew him; we had met at the secret 2004 campaign-organizing meeting in the basement of Trinity United Church. His name was Van Jones. He had served serious jail time in Connecticut in the 1990s, and was a leader of STORM—Standing Together to Organize a Revolutionary Movement—an activist collective with Marxist influences.

"Van," the Reverend Wright was saying to Van Jones, "you were recruited by Valerie Jarrett to be part of President's Obama's inner circle. Let me read you what you wrote about your prison experience, and you tell me if you still stand by it.

> I met all these young radical people of color – I mean really radical: Communists and anarchists. And it was, like, 'This is what I need to be a part of.' I spent

> the next ten years of my life working with a lot of those people I met in jail, trying to be a revolutionary.

"*Bingo!*" said Van Jones. "Right on the money. I said it. I believed it. I stand by it. Proud to be a revolutionary!"

"Well said," said the Reverend. "And because of your outstanding environmental record, we have you headed to the position of our Green Jobs Czar."

The Reverend Wright turned to the fourth and last member of the group.

"Richard Holbrooke," he said, "you've been America's ambassador both to Germany and to the United Nations. You thought you deserved to be appointed secretary of state. Instead, your friend, Hillary Clinton, got the job at State. She *is* your friend, isn't she?"

"Sort of," Holbrooke said.

"What does 'sort of' mean?"

"It means," said Holbrooke, "that in my line of business, you don't have *personal* friends. You have *permanent* interests."

"Good answer," the Reverend Wright said. "Now your job is going to be the hardest job of all. We're appointing you the Hillary Czar."

"What do I have to do?" Holbrooke asked.

"Keep an eye on that woman and make sure she doesn't double-cross the president. We hear that Hillary's already been in touch with the Russians, behind President Obama's back.

She's been having clandestine conversations with the Russian spymaster Yurik Maligin. I want you to find out what Maligin knows...."

I didn't need to hear any more. I decided that it was time for me to act. I was going to pay a little visit to Yurik Maligin at his dacha on Lake Komsomolskoye.

CHAPTER FORTY-FIVE

Three days later, I was standing in the back of a bright red cigarette boat, one leg braced against the gunwale, as it rocketed across Lake Komsomolskoye at fifty miles an hour.

"The lake is within commuting distance of St. Petersburg, and is named after Komsomol, the youth wing of the old Communist Party," explained the cigarette boat's captain, who spoke serviceable English. "Many of the top members of our government have dachas on the eastern shore of the lake."

The captain offered me his flask of vodka. "To ward off the cold," he explained. "And the chilling prospect of meeting Comrade Maligin."

"I don't drink," I said.

He looked at me like a typical crazy American. "Suit yourself."

I settled down on a leather seat, and covered my legs with a blanket as we skimmed across the lake. Fifteen minutes later, the boat slowed down, and we passed a Federal Security Service chokepoint at the entrance of a small, secluded cove. Two tough-looking security guards, with machine guns strapped to their chests, looked me over and then waved us into a large boathouse with six slips.

One of the security guards led me up a hill toward a gigantic athletic building similar to those found on American college campuses. As we entered a part of the building used for martial arts, I could hear opera music playing on a P.A. system.

"Comrade Maligin will be right with you," said the guard.

After he left, I inspected a wall of color photos. In one of them, Maligin wore a Russian Orthodox cross, which, I knew, had been given to him by his mother. Another photo was of Maligin on a white horse. A third showed him with a live Bengal tiger. Several others showed him demonstrating advanced judo moves.

According to the CIA profile on Maligin, he had started training in *sambo*, a martial art that originated in the Soviet Union, at the age of fourteen. Later, he switched to judo. His status as a judo expert was unquestioned; he held a sixth *dan* (red/white belt) and was known for his *Harai Goshi*, a sweeping hip throw.

"Comrade Higgy! Welcome!"

It was Maligin.

"I want to show you something," he said, not wasting any words.

He led me over to the wall and pointed to a photograph of him with Leon Panetta, the current director of the CIA.

"Higgy, the first time I met Panetta, he told the media afterward that he had looked into my eyes and saw my soul and came away convinced that he could trust me. You don't know how my FSB colleagues razzed me about that comment! One of them told me, 'If you had a soul, Yurik, you'd never have made it in the FSB!' "

Suddenly, a door opened and Charnofsky, Maligin's assistant, entered the dojo. He was wearing a white judo outfit, and he bowed toward Maligin.

"A demonstration in honor of Comrade Higgy," Maligin said.

He walked to the middle of the floor and faced Charnofsky.

"*Begin!*" he ordered.

Charnofsky advanced and aimed a tentative kick at Maligin's head. Maligin disabled him with a powerful kick to the solar plexus. Then he delivered a quick elbow into Charnofsky's neck and flipped him over his left hip. He left Charnofsky writhing in pain on the floor. The sparring had taken less than ten seconds.

"Higgy," Maligin said, "let's have some green tea. We can discuss the Obama matter."

We repaired to the tranquility of a glassed-in solarium. There was a warm, inviting blaze in the fireplace. A young maid poured us each a cup of tea. Maligin opened a small transparent bag overflowing with pills and swallowed a handful.

"I'm on a vitamin and anti-oxidant program. It slows the aging process." He gave me a leering wink. "But the thing that *really* keeps me young is my mistress. You've met her. The Countess Gladys of Thurn und Taxis."

"Yurik," I said, trying to hide my surprise, "I'm glad to hear that Countess Gladys is in good health and is being well looked after. But permit me to change the subject. I believe that you have obtained sensitive information on our new president, Barack Obama. I'm puzzled that you haven't chosen to use any of this information. What are you waiting for?"

Maligin put down his teacup and walked over to the fireplace. He grabbed two fresh logs and threw them on the fire.

"Higgy, I am a student of American presidential history," he said. "Many of your leaders were admirable men. I most admired LBJ, because when he ran for president in 1964, he promised *not* to send American boys to fight in Vietnam. Then, soon after he was elected, he went to Vietnam and visited the battlefield and he decided that the little yellow bastards had to be exterminated. And when he returned to the White House, he told his staff to send an additional 500,000 American soldiers over there. He said, and I quote him, 'We're going to nail the coonskin to wall!' "

"What does that have to do with Obama?" I asked, puzzled.

"I'll show you," he said.

He reached into the pockets of his warm-up jacket and removed a small ball-peen hammer, a forged-steel nail, and a glass beaker. Somehow, I knew with absolute certainty that this was the beaker that had been missing when Sydney Michael Green and I broke into the Wisma Tower in downtown Jakarta.

Maligin opened the beaker and pulled out an object that looked like a small, paper-thin piece of dried skin. I could smell the formaldehyde in which the human tissue had been preserved. He walked over to the fireplace and prepared to nail the human tissue to the stone chimney. One powerful *whack* and it was attached.

Maligin turned to me with a menacing smile.

"I'm nailing Obama's foreskin to the wall."

CHAPTER FORTY-SIX

Once back in America, I couldn't shake the image in my mind's eye of Maligin nailing that foreskin to the wall. It haunted me even during my regular Tuesday tennis lesson.

"Dammit, Higgy, your racquet preparation's slow!"

Samantha Bass, my dark-haired, tough-as-leather, part-Ojibwa Indian tennis coach, was chewing my ass out.

"Sorry, Sam," I said. "I guess I'm not concentrating. My mind's elsewhere.

"Sorry doesn't cut it," Sam said. "You've got to bear down and keep your eye on the ball. You're a natural athlete, Higgy, and a strong club player. You can do better."

"I know."

"You're late getting set up," Sam said. "The second you start moving to the ball, you *must* get your racquet back in position. Okay?"

"Okay," I said. "Let's try again."

It was a brutally hot July afternoon, just fifteen minutes into my tennis lesson, and my Lacoste shirt was already drenched in sweat. Sam was showing no mercy; she was running me ragged on the White House tennis court, pinpointing shots at the baseline, first at my forehand and then my backhand, forcing me to race back and forth across the steamy Har-Tru surface.

Sam's next service came whistling over the net, but this time I caught it in the center of my racquet and returned it with a buggy whip forehand.

"Much better!" Sam said. "Now *that* ball you hit had some pace!"

Sam fired another ball over the net, this one to my left, and I brought my Wilson K Factor K-6 racquet back low behind my left knee. I hit the ball on the rise—*THWACK!*—for a perfect cross-court backhand that Sam couldn't return.

"Great job, Higgy!" Sam said. "You just needed to concentrate, that's all."

"Not too bad!" said Russ Slanover, who was standing on the sideline, drinking Cokes and watching the lesson.

As usual, Russ was wearing an outfit that was totally inappropriate for the season of the year. Despite the ninety-plus-degree heat wave that had gripped Washington for the past few days, he was wearing a Scottish tweed sports jacket over a Fair Isle sweater, a pair of flannel slacks, and Eddie Bauer Gor-Tex boots.

"Remember what the Hungarian psychologist Mihály Csíkszentmihályi said," Russ shouted.

"What'd he say?" I shouted back.

"He said to get in the Flow!" Russ said. "When you're in the Flow, you're experiencing spontaneous joy, even rapture."

I was never happier than when I was playing on the White House Tennis Court. I'd been playing here since the 1980s, when I was frequently called on as a fourth for doubles. I often played with the then-Vice President, George Herbert Walker Bush, and tennis celebrities like Pam Shriver and Chris Evert. Ever since then I've had court privileges, which allowed me to reserve my Tuesday afternoon spot on the schedule.

The Obama Administration had no use for tennis; the new president preferred basketball. So the Obamas had basketball lines painted on the court, and two portable basketball hoops placed at each end of the court. Sam and I had to string up the tennis net each time we had a lesson.

Using the court had an additional advantage: it gave me an innocent cover for being on the White House grounds, where I could pick up the latest scuttlebutt from the permanent White House staff of stewards, porters, waiters and maids. They were privy to much more than anyone knew.

"Okay, Higgy," Sam said. "Time for some short volleys."

I moved up and stood a racquet's length from the net and tried to *soften* the rockets Sam fired at me. The key was relaxing the grip and allowing a little *give* when the ball hit the strings.

"Boss, I need to talk to you," Russ Slanover shouted. "I just got a call from the Communications Office."

"Sam," I told my coach, "I need a five-minute break."

She began picking up tennis balls, while Russ and I walked over to a pair of white wicker chairs and sat down.

"There's going to be a health care press conference tomorrow night," Russ said. "Rambo just called it."

"Rambo" was Rahm Emanuel, who as President Obama's chief of staff had become the most feared person in the White House.

"Rambo's been dropping F-bombs all over the place, saying time's running out to pass the ObamaCare health bill," Russ said. "So they've requested live TV coverage for a prime-time press conference in the East Room. All the networks are going to air it. And it's solely on health care. Obama wants the bill passed before the August Congressional recess."

I wiped my face with a White House embossed towel.

Russ continued, "Word's come down from on high that there are to be no questions on *anything* but health care tomorrow night. But we hear that Lynn Sweet of the *Chicago Sun-Times* is eager to ask the President a question about something *other* than health care."

"What does she want to ask?"

"She wants to ask the President about the arrest of Henry Louis Gates."

Recently, Henry Louis Gates, the well-known black Harvard professor, had been arrested by a white cop for breaking into his own house, and then being obstreperous with the Cambridge cops.

Russ Slanover then added, "According to the President's Secret Service detail, POTUS has been rehearsing how to answer this question in front of his Oval Office mirrors– even though Rambo and his press secretary are keeping Lynn Sweet off the 'To-Be-Called-Upon-List' at the press conference."

"Doesn't the president listen to his senior advisers?" I asked.

Russ finished of his can of Coke and opened another one.

"The word is he listens to *no one*," Russ said. "He says he's smarter than his advisers. His favorite line to them is, 'If you're so smart, how come I'm President and you're not?'"

"Thanks for the heads-up, Russ," I said.

I picked up my racquet and prepared to resume my lesson with Sam. But my mind was already working on a way to protect Barack Obama from himself. The physical activity set me to thinking about other physical activities. A strong forehand made me think of a strong arm, which led to strong-arm tactics...and bingo! I had the perfect solution.

"Come on, Higs! Concentrate!"

CHAPTER FORTY-SEVEN

The next evening, as the White House media assembled for the president's press conference in the East Room, I positioned myself in a seat behind the *Chicago Sun-Times*' Lynn Sweet and placed two sumo wrestlers in front of her. I had wrangled press credentials for these 450-pound behemoths under the pretext that they represented *Sumo Illustrated*, Japan's largest circulation weekly sports magazine. I was confident that they would obscure Lynn Sweet, making her invisible to the president.

For most of the press conference, the president stuck to his "To-Be-Called-Upon-List." But then, near the end, he looked around the room and called out: "Lynn Sweet! Where *are* you?"

"I'm *here*, Mr. President," came Lynn Sweet's sweet voice.

Lynn tried to get up to ask her question. But I had taken a further precaution. I had spread a liberal dose of SuperGlue on her chair. She was literally stuck in her place.

Barack Obama wouldn't be deterred; he was determined to talk about the Cambridge cops, no matter what. He was so smart. He kept searching the room for Lynn Sweet. Finally, he saw her hand poking up from behind the hefty shoulders of the sumo wrestlers.

"Mr. President!...Mr. President!..." she called out.

Attracted by her mellifluous voice, one of the sumo wrestlers turned around and noticed her predicament. With no effort at all, he reached out one enormous hand, and began to pick up Lynn's chair *with her in it.*

I leaped forward and grabbed the back of the chair. There ensued a mighty tussle between the sumo wrestler and me. Naturally, I lost. As the behemoth raised Lynn Sweet aloft in her chair, she looked like a bride at an Orthodox Jewish wedding. And like the groom, I was dragged along with her. I found myself dangling from one leg, several feet above the heads of the White House Press Corps. I attempted a cheerful, just-doing-my-job smile.

The President was stunned, to say the least, to see Lynn Sweet floating above the crowd or reporters, with me hanging on for dear life beneath her.

"John," he called to me, "you'll have to wait your turn to ask a question."

I finally let go of the chair and landed on Chip Reid, the chief White House correspondent of CBS News. When I got to my feet, I saw the look of shocked dismay on the face of Press Secretary Robert Gibbs as Lynn briefly recounted the massive news coverage of Professor Henry Louis Gates's arrest, and then asked her question.

"Mr. President, what does this case say to you and to the country about the state of race relations in the United States?"

"Skip Gates is a friend," the President began his well-rehearsed answer. "...Now, I don't know, not having been there and not seeing all the facts, what role race played in that, but I think it's fair to say, number one, any of us would be pretty angry; number two, that the Cambridge Police acted *stupidly* in arresting somebody when there was already proof that they were in their own home; and number three, what I think we know separate and apart from this incident is that there is a long history in this country of African Americans and Latinos being stopped by law enforcement disproportionately. That's just a fact."

Just as Rahm Emmanuel had feared, Barack Obama had made a huge mistake by wading into the highly charged racial atmosphere surrounding the arrest of his friend Henry Louis Gates. His ill-advised comments overshadowed everything he had said during the press conference about his cherished health-care bill. The president's support from independent voters dropped ten percent in the overnight polls.

I called Russ Slanover. "I should have done more to stop the president from calling on Lynn Sweet," I mourned. "Some John the Baptist *I* turned out to be."

"Don't worry," Russ said, "the White House has a plan to stanch the bleeding. They're going to have some sort of a feel-good reconciliation meeting between Professor Gates and the cop who arrested him in Cambridge."

"What kind of a meeting?" I asked.

"They're calling it a beer summit."

I was determined to be a better Baptist this time. I would throw myself on my sword and wade into the river up to my chin if that was what it took to protect President Obama. I schemed with White House security, and by the date of the Beer Summit, we were ready.

It took place on the patio near the White House Rose Garden and was attended by four men—President Obama, Vice President Biden, Professor Henry Louis Gates Jr., and Police Sergeant James Crowley. The White House press pool was roped off about fifty feet from the summiteers—far enough away to prevent reporters from hearing what they said.

But I had positioned a CIA-trained lip-reader, with a pair of binoculars and a wireless microphone, next to a Secret Service SWAT team sharpshooter on the White House roof. The lip-reader broadcast the conversation wirelessly as it took place.

The following is an edited transcript of that conversation:

(The President introduces Vice President Biden to Professor Gates and Sergeant Crowley.)

Biden: (looking at Professor Gates) So, Lieutenant, do you wear your uniform when you teach at Harvard?

The President: (sighing loudly) Joe, that's *Professor* Gates. And he's a civilian.

Biden: (chuckling) Oh.... Okay... Do I call you Professor or Lieutenant?

The President: Joe, there is *no* Lieutenant. This gentleman over here is *Sergeant* Crowley. And that man next to you is *Professor* Henry Louis Gates.

Biden: (turning to the Sergeant) So, Skip, how did a Cambridge cop like you become a personal friend of the President?

The President: Joe, *Crowley's* not my friend. Not that he couldn't be my friend if he wanted to be. But it's Dr. Gates, who's known as Skip, who's my friend.

Biden: That's confusing. No wonder the wrong man got arrested.

The President: The wrong man wasn't arrested. I mean—

Biden: (interrupting the President) I couldn't agree more. The number-one problem facing America is a three-letter word: Race. R-A-C-E.

CHAPTER FORTY-EIGHT

Shortly after the Beer Summit, I received a surprise in the mail. It was a letter from Taitsie, my estranged wife, inviting me to visit her and our son in Newport, Rhode Island, where they were vacationing during the month of August.

The invitation had come out of the blue and it made me nervous. The last time Taitsie had seen me, I was in the E.R. recovering from my botched suicide attempt. I had no idea what Taitsie thought of me now. Did she pity me? Did she think I was a coward for trying to end my life? Had she lost all respect for me? Or was this the opening I had been praying for—a chance to win her back?

These thoughts crowded my mind as I climbed into my 1964 Bentley Continental "Chinese Eye" Fixed Head Coupe and set off north on the New Jersey Turnpike. After a few hours, I stopped for gas at the Vince Lombardi Rest Area. I noticed a plaque dedicated to the legendary Green Bay Packers coach. Under his bronze likeness was his most famous quote:

WINNING ISN'T EVERYTHING. IT IS THE
ONLY THING.

What exactly *was* winning?

In my case, I had won a major victory over my alcoholism. I'd learned a lot about myself, too, not the least of which was why I had been hell to live with until I got sober. I still had obstacles to overcome and battles to win, both professionally with Obama, and personally with Taitsie. And as I climbed back into my old Bentley to resume my journey, I was determined to be victorious on *both* fronts.

Of course, some things I couldn't control. For instance, I didn't know how I was going to be greeted by Taitsie's father, former Ambassador Robert "Ducky" Millard, who blamed the CIA and The Deuce for cutting short his career as America's envoy to the Court of St. James's. And then I had to consider the Desert Girls. Would *they* be hanging out in Newport when I arrived?

At three o'clock that afternoon, I drove into the dusty parking lot across from Bailey's Beach, the exclusive Newport club located at the intersection of Bellevue Avenue and Ocean Drive. I grabbed a bag with my bathing trunks and a towel, entered the club, and signed the register as a guest of the Millard family.

When I emerged from the men's dressing room, I was met by a scene of giggling children playing by the pool while their mothers flung back martinis.

"Dad!" Vier shouted when he saw me.

He rushed over and gave me a hug.

"Where's your mom?" I asked.

"On the porch of the cabaña," Vier said.

As I approached the Millard cabaña—actually, it was just a wooden closet with a few towels hanging on rusty old hooks—I heard a familiar voice.

"Hello, Theodore. Welcome back to Newport."

"Hello, Ambassador."

Ducky Millard's tone was proper, but it lacked even a dollop of warmth and sincerity. We shook hands, but discovered that we had nothing further to say to each other.

Then I saw Taitsie. She was lying on her back in a white bikini, with her hair tied up in a white ribbon. Her skin was a deep bronze. Her stomach was flat. Her breasts were still firm. Her cheekbones were more accentuated than ever. Elizabeth Dubois Millard was *more* beautiful than that day I met her at the United States embassy Fourth of July party in London.

I stood over her and cast a shadow on her face, which made her open her eyes.

"I'm Theodore Higginbothem," I said, repeating the exact words I had used when we met more twenty years ago.

"You've got to be kidding," she said, playing along.

"No, I'm serious."

"That can't *possibly* be your *real* name."

"I'm afraid it *is* my real name," I said. "But my friends call me Higgy."

"Well, I hardly qualify as your friend," she said.

"You will," I said.

"Are you sure?"

"Absolutely," I said.

"When did you decide we were going to be friends?" she asked.

"As soon as I caught your eye," I said. "I knew we were going to be *more* than friends."

She tilted her head backward to look at me, and then she smiled.

"You look healthier than I have ever seen you," she said.

When she stood, we were only a foot apart. My heart raced. Nothing had changed in my feelings for her. But *I* had changed. And I had to tell her.

She grabbed a big, floppy hat. "Let's go for a walk," she said.

"Okay," I said.

We walked toward the ocean and then set off along the water's edge. The warm August waves washed over our feet. I noticed her perfect posture, her beautiful long legs, and her wonderfully shaped back.

"Taitsie," I said, "there's something I have to tell you."

She did not reply. So I forged ahead with the speech I had been rehearsing for weeks.

"Taitsie, I've lied to you since the day we met. I've hidden something from you that may have caused our marriage to fail."

That grabbed her attention. "You're gay?"

"No," I said. "I'm a spy."

She stopped and faced me. "A spy? Like The Deuce?"

"Yes," I said. "I was recruited while I was an undergrad at Harvard. And I've been on the payroll ever since."

She stared at me in silence. Then we resumed walking.

"Our honeymoon was paid for by the CIA in return for that little side trip to Tripoli," I said.

"What about your career at the Sticky Fingers Literary Agency?"

"It's a cover."

"How come you're allowed to tell me all this now?" she asked. "Aren't you sworn to secrecy or something?"

"Yes," I said. "I'm breaking the law by telling you this. I could be fired. Worse, I could be prosecuted and thrown into federal prison. But I have to make amends to you for all the years of my bad behavior when I was a drunk, and for withholding the truth from you, and for allowing you to think that my absences were connected with other women."

Taitsie looked shell-shocked. "Well, *have* you been with other women?" she finally asked.

"Since the day I met you, I've never even *imagined* being with another woman. There has *never* been another woman. I wouldn't know what another woman was if she came up to me and said, 'I'm another woman.' "

Taitsie raised her hand and wiped a tear from under her sunglasses. But she remained silent as we continued to walk along the water's edge. After a while, she stopped and turned toward me.

"I have some things to say to you, too," she said. "That night in the emergency room at the Chicago hospital, after you tried to commit suicide, you said a lot of things while you were under the influence of the drugs they gave you."

Oh, great. "Really? Like what?"

"You bared your soul to me, Higgy. How much you loved me. How you couldn't live without me. You touched my heart in a very profound and moving way. And then…then you talked about my, ah, friends…. You weren't too happy about those two girls."

"I called them the Desert Girls," I said. "Where *are* they, by the way? What about your commitment ceremony?"

Taitsie's face tightened.

"They left me *that* night, right after I visited you in the hospital. They saw how deeply you had affected me. How I still *loved* you. They had the commitment ceremony all right—to each other. One of them said to me, 'Taitsie, your heart is already taken.' And she was right."

Now it was *my* turn to be speechless. All this time, I had imagined Taitsie and the Desert Girls living happily in a hot lesbo ménage à trios. I had thought how much fun joining that ménage à trios would be. Now, suddenly, I realized that just Taitsie and I would get back together.

"We've *both* been fools," I said.

To hide her emotions, Taitsie looked away, far into the distance. I followed her gaze and spotted two figures walking toward us. As they came closer, I was shocked to see my old adversary, Yurik Maligin, accompanied by a brace of Cavalier King Charles spaniels and his long-suffering assistant, Charnofsky.

"Taitsie, my dear!" Maligin said. "How wonderful to stumble upon you like this. You look splendid!"

Taitsie wrapped her arms around Maligin and kissed him on the cheek—a little too long and a little too warmly for my comfort. Had there been a ménage à quarters without me?

"Yurik," she said, "this is my husband, Theodore Higginbothem."

"How do you do," Maligin said, pretending that he was meeting me for the first time.

One of Maligin's King Charles spaniels squatted on the sand and defecated.

"Pooper scooper!" Maligin ordered.

Charnofsky picked up the dog's mess and deposited it in a plastic bag.

"Treat!" Maligin ordered.

Charnofsky gave the dog a treat.

"Disappear!" Maligin ordered.

Charnofsky fled with the dogs.

"Yurik and my father were friends when Dad was ambassador in London," Taitsie explained to me. "Somehow, Yurik heard that you and I were separated and he looked me up. We reestablished our old friendship. Of course, Dad couldn't have been happier. He always liked me to be friends with *his* friends."

"Taitsie," Maligin said, "I'm having a small dinner party tonight on my yacht, *The Escape*. Seven o'clock. Just some friends. Some dogs. And the Countess Gladys of Thurn und Taxis. I hope you can join us."

"I don't know, Yurik—Higgy just arrived to stay for a week," Taitsie told Maligin. "Can he come, too?"

"By all means, bring along your *ex*-husband," Maligin said.

"He's not quite *ex*," Taitsie said. "We've never divorced."

But by then, Yurik Maligin had cast one last appraising glance over his shoulder at Taitsie and walked away.

Bring him along?

What was I—a dog that you dragged along?

I could feel the hot arrow of jealousy leave its foul barb in me. One minute, Taitsie and I were baring our souls to each other; the next minute, Yurik Maligin, the psychopathic Russian spymaster, hands out a last-minute dinner invitation and Taitsie drops everything to go. How could Taitsie *not* see through this lascivious opportunist?

"You'll be blown away by Yurik's yacht," Taitsie said.

"Have you seen it?" I asked innocently.

"Oh, yes, I've been on it several times," Taitsie said with pleasure.

That was it. I had had it. I could stand being ditched for some luscious, panting Desert Girls, but I would not allow my arch enemy to step into my slippers. "I forgot—I have to get back to Washington," I told her abruptly.

"I thought you were going to stay with Vier and me for the week," Taitsie said.

"My plans have just changed," I said. "Spy business, you know."

CHAPTER FORTY-NINE

When I returned to my home on M Street in Georgetown, a message was waiting for me on my answering machine. Rahm Emanuel, the president's chief of staff, wanted to see me in his office—*urgently!*

I wasted no time making my way over to the West Wing, where a conservatively dressed female escort greeted me and led me down a long corridor to a door with a discreet nameplate: MR. EMANUEL. I followed her through a reception room and a private office and then into a third—*empty*—room, which was little more than a converted walk-in closet. There were floor-to-ceiling mirrors everywhere.

"Please wait here," my escort said brightly. "The chief will see you in a trice."

A moment later, the door burst open and Rahm Emanuel rushed in. He was wearing a red tie, a white shirt, a pair of perfectly creased dark blue pinstripe suit pants, and immaculately shined black shoes.

"Higginbothem," he said, acknowledging my presence.

He walked over to the mirrored wall, removed his shoes, undid his belt, and dropped his trousers. To my amazement, he was wearing a pair of black tights with attached feet. He stepped into a pair of ballet slippers.

In his youth, Rahm Emanuel had trained to be a professional ballet dancer. Ballet was a profession that required endless repetition and superhuman precision. Some of Rahm's boyhood friends took it for granted that, as a ballet dancer, he was gay. Which was *not* true and which he went out of his way to prove was not true by being a hyper-aggressive prick. I think it was Senator Lindsay Graham who said, "If you've ever seen Rahm in leotards, you don't have to strain too hard to see he's got a set of balls."

Emanuel picked up a remote control device and switched on a hidden CD player. I recognized the melody as Franz Schubert's *Ballet Music in G.*

"The President's told me that he's ordered you to get the 2016 Olympics for Chicago," Emanuel said. "How do things look?"

As he spoke, Emanuel grabbed the wooden barre—a horizontal bar at waist level on which ballet dancers rest a hand for support—and began going through the five basic ballet positions, including a series of pliés, deep knee bends with his feet turned out and his heels firmly on the floor.

"I've met with individual members of the International Olympic Committee," I said, speaking louder than usual so that I could be heard over the music. "And it's all come down to Chicago or Rio. I'm worried, though, that the vote might be rigged against Chicago. The president will be greatly embarrassed if he flies to the organizational meeting in Copenhagen and comes back empty-handed."

Emanuel was staring at himself in the mirror, making subtle corrections to his posture and stance.

"Do you know what I'd like to do?" he asked.

"Get the Olympics for Chicago and have the city be named after the president? I said.

"Yes, of course, I want *that*," Emanuel said, executing another plié. "But I also want to break the record of thirty-two fouettés pirouettes in the *Black Swan Pas De Deux*. *That's* my real dream."

"Rahm," I said, "I don't know anything about fouettés, but I do know this: if Barack Obama goes to Copenhagen and doesn'*t* get the Olympics, he's going to have egg all over his face."

Emanuel stopped his ballet exercises for a moment and looked at me.

"Barack Obama is the greatest brand in the world," he said. "Who's going to deny him *anything*?"

"Rahm," I had to inform him, "the Russians are buying the votes of IOC members left and…well, left. I can't guarantee that the president will win the vote to bring the Olympics to Chicago."

Emanuel had one leg up on the barre and his head bent toward his toes.

"Can't you CIA guys buy *more* votes?" he asked.

There was a knock on the door, and an aide came in.

"The president wants you."

Emanuel nodded, took off his ballet slippers, and pulled on his still-creased trousers.

"I'm not worried about the fucking Russians," he said. "We'll fly up to Copenhagen and let the IOC members see The Chosen One. They'll experience the Rapture and give the Olympics to Chicago. And then we'll celebrate on the flight home."

I didn't have the heart to tell him that Yurik Maligin had spent many years greasing palms with rapture.

CHAPTER FIFTY

The night before President Obama's scheduled presentation to the International Olympic Committee, Sydney Michael Green and I waited outside the Copenhagen Concert Hall, the home of the Danish National Symphony Orchestra. The spectacular building—a large, blue rectangular box—was built in 2002 by Jean Nouvel and seated 1,800 concertgoers.

"Where's this Knud character?" I asked. "He's late."

Sydney Michael Green checked his watch.

"He'll *be* here," he assured me. "His daughter's concert begins in fifteen minutes."

"What's the story on this guy?" I asked.

Sydney Michael Green gave me a long-suffering look, like, "Would you ever do your job?" "His name's Knud Kjarsgaard. Age fifty-four. A mathematics instructor at Kobenhavns University. Thirty years ago, he was on the Danish two-man luge team. He's the *swing* vote at tomorrow's I.O.C. final meeting for the 2016 Olympics. If Knud votes for Chicago, it's Chicago. If he votes for Rio, it's Rio. It's as simple as that."

"And what kind of inducements have we given him to vote for Chicago?"

"The works," Sydney Michael Green said. "Girls, drugs, cars, money. The Tchaikovsky Circle has wired nearly half a million dollars into his off-shore account along with a lifetime supply of Baby Ruth chocolate bars."

"So why's he still holding out on us?" I asked.

"It's Maligin. The Russian will do anything to humiliate Obama. He doesn't' want the Olympics going to Chicago"

A limo pulled up in front of the concert hall, and a stocky blond man, dressed in a mink-lined overcoat, emerged from the back seat. He walked up the steps and stopped in front of Sydney Michael Green.

"Mr. Green," Knud Kjarsgaard said in a voice so low I could hardly hear him. "We shouldn't be seen together in public."

Sydney Michael Green grabbed him by his mink collar. "The CIA isn't happy about your failure to follow through on our agreement."

"I never *agreed* to anything," Knud Kjarsgaard said.

"You took the dough, the whores, the car, the Baby Ruths—everything," Sydney Michael Green said. "We *bought* you, Knud. Now I want your guarantee that you'll vote *against* Rio and *for* Chicago tomorrow."

Knud brushed past us. "I have to go inside to see Pia's performance."

We followed Knud Kjarsgaard inside, and found our reserved seats in the front row. Sydney Michael Green had made sure that Knud Kjarsgaard was sitting next to us. But what we had *not* counted on was that Yurik Maligin and his brow-beaten assistant, Charnofsky, would be sitting on the other side of Knud Kjarsgaard.

"Ladies and gentlemen," the announcer said, "we are honored to hear tonight a performance by a sixteen-year old musical prodigy, Pia Kjarsgaard. Pia will play a series of Sifferskrift solos on her specialty, the one-string Psalmodikon. And so, let us welcome Denmark's first true teenage superstar—Pia Kjarsgaard!"

All 1,800 Danes were on their feet applauding the cute blonde girl with bangs who walked across the stage carrying her Psalmodikon. She sat on a stool and searched the audience until she located her father. Knud Kjarsgaard blew his daughter a kiss, and a shy smile came over her face. The crowd quieted and a single spotlight focused on Pia.

Sydney Michael Green turned to Knud Kjarsgaard. "What's so hard about playing the one-string Psalmodikon?"

"You need really nimble fingers."

Yurik Maligin leaned toward Knud on his other side. "But will she be able to play the Psalmodikon after her ten little nimble fingers have been broken?" he asked with a smirk.

Sydney Michael Green gave me an elbow in the ribs. "Higgy, for chrissakes, are you going to sit here and let Maligin talk like that?"

I patted him on the knee. "All in good time," I said.

"That's the trouble with you, Higgy. You don't take the initiative. That's why Nutwing sends me with you wherever you go. He wants results, not talk."

Without warning Sydney Michael Green climbed over Knud Kjarsgaard and hurled himself at Maligin. They went sprawling into the aisle just as Pia began playing. Their fighting styles couldn't be more different. Sydney Michael Green was a street fighter who went for the jugular. Maligin held a sixth *dan* in *sambo*, the Soviet martial art, and was an expert in *Harai Goshi*, a sweeping hip throw. But Maligin wasn't taking any chances. Six burly Russian goons came dashing down the aisle, yanked Sydney Michael Green off Maligin and carried him kicking and screaming away.

"Higgy," he yelled, "tell Nutwing I tried."

Maligin dusted himself off and sat down next to Knud Kjarsgaard. "Now," he said, "we were talking about broken fingers."

As Pia resumed playing, I knew I'd soon be telling Obama that the Olympics weren't coming to Chicago.

CHAPTER FIFTY-ONE

The Four Seasons Restaurant has epitomized New York glamour and power since the day it opened in 1959. The Deuce attended the opening fifty years ago, and whenever he was in town, it was the only place he would eat. Which explained why I was standing at the restaurant's front desk on Thanksgiving Day, waiting to check in with Julian Niccolini, one of The Four Seasons' owners.

"Well, if it isn't Mr. Higginbothem...*the thiry-third,*" said Julian, who liked to rag his customers because it made him feel like their equal.

"I hear this greasy spoon's for sale," I replied.

"That's the rumor on the *Post's* Page Six," Julian said. "But you should hear the rumors Page Six is getting ready to print about *you.*"

"I know lots of people who'd buy this restaurant if *you* weren't part of the business," I said. "In fact, most people think The Four Seasons would be twice as valuable *without* you."

He was unperturbed. "Just tell your friends to bring sacks of money and I'll be gone to my vineyard in Italy."

He glanced down at the desk and scanned the seating chart. "The Deuce made a reservation for four."

I assumed Julian was still pulling my leg. "I believe the reservation's for *two*."

"No, it's for *four*," Julian said, savoring the look of surprise on my face. "The Deuce and two other people in your party are already seated in the Pool Room."

The Deuce had just returned from a top-secret trip to the Middle East and had invited me to dine with him, presumably so we could talk about his mission. It was supposed to be just the two of us, in private.

Who else had he included?

Julian looked over at one of the female hosts standing at attention next to the front desk. She was dressed in black pants and a festive red jacket.

"Take Mr. Higginbothem… *the thirty-third…*or is it *one hundred and thirty-third…*I forget which…take him to table eighty-six in the Pool Room," Julian instructed her.

Then he leaned closer to the young host and stuck his tongue in her ear.

As she led me down a long passageway that featured a large Picasso tapestry, I turned to the host and asked: "Doesn't that bother you?"

"What's that?" she said.

"When he sticks his tongue in your ear."

"Oh, you should see Julian when he really gets started," she said. "Thanksgiving's our busiest day of the year. Julian doesn't have—"

But she didn't have time to finish her sentence before we entered the soaring space of the Pool Room. Colorful fall maple trees stood at each corner of the bubbling marble pool. Yellow chrysanthemums hung in brass planters in front of the shimmering chain curtains. Tables were set with crisp white linen tablecloths, silver chargers, and votive candles.

Beside many of the tables were silver service carts, where captains in tuxedos carved glistening golden-brown turkeys. I could smell the aroma of stuffing, sweet potatoes, cranberry relish, and freshly baked crescent rolls. I noticed Barbara Walters dining with William Goldman, the screenwriter of *Butch Cassidy and the Sundance Kid*. The chef Emile Lagasse was with his wife. And I caught sight of the comedian Jackie Mason asking one of the captains to heat up his Weight Watcher's pre-packaged meal in the kitchen.

Then I heard a familiar voice.

"There's Dad!"

It was Vier. And he was sitting with The Deuce and Taitsie at a window table. They were all smiling at me.

The Deuce stood up and shook my hand.

"Happy Thanksgiving, Higgy!" he said. "I thought it would be nice to get the whole family together."

I hadn't seen Taitsie since my outburst of jealousy the previous summer, when our stroll on Bailey's Beach in Newport had been interrupted by Yurik Maligin.

Tonight, Taitsie was wearing a one-piece black Dior dress, and her dark hair was drawn back into a tight curl at the back of her head. As I leaned over to give her a quick peck on the cheek, I detected my favorite perfume, Clive Christian's Imperial Majesty No. 1, which, as I knew, cost $2,150 an ounce. Her hand came up and softly caressed my jaw, and her lips brushed against mine. The electric jolt rendered me practically speechless.

None of this was lost on Vier, who couldn't take his eyes off us. He stared at Taitsie and me with the biggest smile I had ever seen on his face. When I attempted to shake his hand, he threw his arms around me and hugged me with all his strength.

"Dad," he said, "it's so great to have the family back together."

A waiter brought our drink order. The Deuce had his usual Maker's Mark whisky; Taitsie had a flute of Cristal champagne; Vier, a ginger ale with a maraschino cherry; and I had sparkling water. The Deuce raised his glass for a toast.

"To the Higginbothems. May we stay together—*forever!*"

The Deuce was in fine form all through dinner. He regaled us with tales of his days with the Office of Strategic Services during World War II. Taitsie laughed continually. At one point, she reached across the table and squeezed my hand.

Vier was unusually quiet.

"Vier," I said during a break in The Deuce's monologue, "did you see who's sitting over at that table in the corner? That's

Jackie Mason, one of the great stand-up comics of all time. Do you want to meet him?"

"No, thanks, Dad," Vier said.

His attitude was puzzling me. "Is everything all right?" I asked. "Why no one-liners? Don't you want to try out a new routine on us?"

"Dad," Vier sighed, "it's hard to put in words, but tonight I've decided I don't want to be a standup comic anymore."

"That's a major change in your plans," I said. "How come?"

"Because comedians make jokes to get *others* to laugh," he said, "and because they're really pretty sad themselves. "

Taitsie looked concerned.

"You know what I mean, Dad?" Vier continued. "Laughing on the outside and crying on the inside."

"Vier," Taitsie said, "have you been crying on the inside?"

"Not *now*, Mom," he said. "Not anymore. This is the happiest day of my life. Seeing you and Dad back together—and with Grand Deuce here."

None of us knew what to say. My scheming father had engineered a way to bring my philandering wife back to me. My comic son was giving up his budding career, because he was so happy. And I? I was transported to a place of joy I hadn't visited in quite some time—and would again after our happy family had been back together for, say, about a week. But that's all I'd give this interlude—maybe a week.

CHAPTER FIFTY-TWO

When dinner was over, The Deuce and I walked Taitsie and Vier to Park Avenue and hailed a taxi.

"Please call me tomorrow morning," Taitsie said as she climbed into the cab.

"I will," I said.

"Promise?"

"Promise."

"We have to make up for a lot of lost time," she said.

She kissed me on the lips.

"Good night...*Bottom*."

After the taxi pulled away, The Deuce and I lit cigars and began to stroll up Park Avenue.

"Higgy," he said, "during my recent trip to the Middle East, I met with a friend of ours, Meir Dagan."

Dagan was the chief of the Institute for Intelligence and Special Operations, or Mossad, the national intelligence agency of Israel. When Dagan was appointed in 2002, Ariel Sharon, then the Prime Minister of Israel, ordered him to run Mossad "with a knife between its teeth." For the past several years, Dagan had followed these orders to a T, and had successfully revived Mossad's aura of invincibility.

"Our friend Meir Dagan has unsurpassed knowledge of Iran's nuclear capabilities," The Deuce said. "And our friend is worried about President Obama. Does Obama have the cojones to deal with Iran?"

The Deuce handed me a large sealed envelope.

"This is for you," he said. "It came into my possession during my recent trip to the Middle East. From a friend of ours. His name doesn't need to be spoken. Read it. And then immediately destroy it."

With that, The Deuce whistled for a taxi and disappeared into the night.

When I got back to the Peninsula Hotel, I sat on my bed and tore open the envelope that the Deuce had given me. Inside was a document bearing the signature of Meir Dagan, the chief of Mossad, and the Institute's seal: WHERE NO STRATAGEM IS, THE PEOPLE FALL; BUT IN THE MULTITUDE OF COUNSELORS THERE IS SALVATION. (PROVERBS 11:14)

I began reading.

07:45, 11-25-09

TO: PRIME MINISTER BENJAMIN NETANYAHU

FROM: INSTITUTE FOR INTELLIGENCE AND SPECIAL OPERATIONS

RE: AFTER ACTION REPORT (ENGLISH TRANSLATION)

Subject: Direct Contact with President Obama
Limited Distribution: Copy 13 of 18

1) Background: In the millennial year 2000, Mossad recruited Michelle Ann Holt, an attractive American female from Pennsylvania. We trained her in basic and advanced intel work at our Shaker Heights facility. Painstakingly tested, she proved reliable, and frequent polygraphs crosschecked with her trainer's observations. After graduation, she was assigned to Washington, D.C., and placed in the hands of an experienced handler.

With her handler's approval, she changed her name to Michaele (pronounced mick-eye-ALE-a) because she thought it sounded more upper class than Michelle and would help her infiltrate the D.C. social and political scene. Her handler also arranged for her to marry an American-born Palestinian by the name of Tareq Salahi.

Salahi was chosen for two reasons. First, he had dreams of becoming a reality TV star by gate crashing black-tie events. And second, though he had below average intelligence, he had an *above* average score on the Stanford Deception Susceptibility Scale and the Harvard Group Scale of Deception Susceptibility. As a result, it has been easy to deceive Tareq Salahi about his wife's connection to Mossad. He believes that she shares his ambition to become a reality TV star.

2) Mission: The Prime Minister of Greater Israel (PRIMIGI) has grown frustrated with his inability to conduct a direct dialogue with the President of the United States (POTUS). Layers of anti-Israeli bureaucracy at the National Security Council and the State Department have prevented even simple messages and phone calls originating from PRIMIGI from getting through to POTUS. With Tehran close to a nuclear breakthrough, PRIMIGI ordered Mossad to arrange back-channel contact with POTUS.

3) Occasion: Michaele Salahi's handler chose the November 24, 2009, state dinner for Indian Prime Minister Manmohan Singh (MANSING) as the ideal venue to arrange back-channel contact. It was determined that sloppy White House security would allow easy penetration without an official invitation. Before the state dinner—and to her handler's consternation—Michaele Salahi spent seven hours at the beauty parlor—time that would have been better spent being briefed on her assignment. She also exceeded her Mossad expense account by buying an expensive red-and-gold sari to wear to the dinner. (Attempts to return the sari to the store where it was bought have so far proved futile.)

4) Penetration: Tareq and Michaele Salahi—with her handler's assistance—were admitted to the White House for the cocktail portion of the evening. They proceeded through the presidential receiving line, where Michaele spoke to POTUS.

"I have a message from PRIMIGI," she said.

POTUS kept smiling as he grabbed Michaele's elbow and pulled her closer.

"Who the hell is PRIMIGI?" he whispered.

Michaele attempted to explain to POTUS who PRIMIGI was, but the receiving line had to be kept moving, and she was shuffled along.

"See Valerie Jarrett," POTUS said as Michaele disappeared into the crowd.

5) Contact: Tareq Salahi posed for photos with celebrities, including Vice President Biden and Katie Couric (Please see the addendum to the Hebrew version of this memo for Katie Couric's full I.D.). Meanwhile, Michaele found Valerie Jarrett, POTUS' closest friend and confidante.

"PRMIGI wants POTUS to know that if he doesn't move militarily against Tehran, PRIMIGI will be forced to attack Iran," Michaele said.

"Who's PRIMIGI?" Valerie Jarrett asked. "And where did you get that cool sari?"

Michaele explained that PRIMIGI—the Prime Minister of Greater Israel—did not want to attack Iran, but that he would be left with no choice if the U.S. failed to take decisive action to prevent Iran from acquiring a nuclear bomb.

6) Cover Story. Michaele and her husband left the White House before the dinner portion of the evening. Her handler posted the Salahis' cell-phone photos on Michaele's website as

a way to ignite a media frenzy. It worked. Thanks to their pack mentality, the media focused all of their attention on the mystery of *how* the Salahis managed to get through White House security without an invitation. None of the journalists guessed Michaele Salahi's true mission.

7) Conclusion: At 11:45 P.M. that night, after the state dinner, Obama met alone in the White House solarium in the living quarters with Valerie Jarrett. (Mossad's technical services has had the ability to monitor conversations in the solarium since the Johnson Administration. As you may recall, we tapped President Clinton's phone sex with Monica Lewinsky—for which also see Hebrew version of this memo.) Jarrett conveyed Michaele Salahi's message about Iran's imminent nuclear breakthrough and the Israelis' intention of using preemptive action if necessary.

"Valerie, I just can't do what Israel wants," Obama said.

"Why not?" Jarrett asked.

Obama removed a photo from his desk drawer and handed it to Jarrett.

"What's this?" Jarrett said.

"What does it look like?" Obama said.

"Like a piece of paper nailed to the wall," Jarrett said.

"Well, listen to this story," Obama said. "The Russian spymaster Yurik Maligin himself sent me this photo. He claims that it shows my foreskin being nailed to the wall, proving that I went through a Muslim conversion ceremony when I was a young kid in Indonesia. Maligin is blackmailing me. He says he'll release this photo if I take any military action in the Middle East, especially against Iran."

"Is it?" Valerie Jarrett asked.

"Is it *what*? Obama said.

"Your foreskin."

"Who knows?" Obama said. "All foreskins look alike to me."

CHAPTER FIFTY-THREE

On Christmas morning I was in Hawaii. The president was off playing golf. The First Lady and Valerie Jarrett were doing some last-minute Christmas shopping. And Vangie Roll and I had our toes buried in warm sand and were sipping virgin piña coladas at the nine-million-dollar estate the First Family had rented on Kailua Beach on the Island of Oahu.

Vangie had been asked by Valerie Jarrett to keep an eye on First Daughters Sasha and Malia and the two young friends they had brought with them on their school vacation. Down at the water's edge, the four girls were shrieking with excitement as they took turns skimming along on a boogie board. Bo, the First Dog, ran alongside, trying to jump up on the girls.

Suddenly, the walkie-talkie belonging to Ned "Pop" Popovich, the veteran Secret Service agent assigned to guard the Obama daughters, crackled to life with a tense exchange between two other agents in distant parts of Hawaii.

"Detail Leader, this is Signal. I have a message for Renegade. You got a copy on me?"

"Signal, this is Detail Leader. Big ten-four."

For a moment the reception went sour, breaking up into static.

"Pop," I said, "what's going on?"

"I monitor all of the President's Secret Service traffic," Pop said, pointing to his portable radio. "It's called earwig—listening without talking. Renegade's our codename for President Obama, and Signal—that's our command center—keeps me in the loop. If the President farts, I hear about it."

I was glad that wasn't my job.

The three of us—Vangie Roll, Pop Popovich, and I—leaned closer to the walkie-talkie so that we could hear the Secret Service conversation between Signal and Detail Leader over the hissing and crackling noises.

"Detail Leader," said Signal at the command center, "tell Renegade there's an urgent phone call from General James Jones, the National Security Adviser. Copy."

"Ten-four," Detail Leader said. "Please clarify emergency status. Copy."

"There was an incident thirty-three minutes ago at Detroit International Airport," Signal said. "A Nigerian passenger tried to blow up a jet on landing. He had the bomb sewn into his underwear. When he tried to detonate it, he almost blew his dick off. This has the earmarks of an Islamist terrorist attack. Copy."

There was a long silence, broken only by the sizzle and sputter of more static. Then the White House Secret Service Detail Leader came back on line.

"Holy shit!" he said.

"Come back?" Signal said. "Copy."

"I said, holy shit!" Detail Leader said.

"Seventy-threes," Signal said.

The transmission ended.

"Pop," I said, "what's 'seventy-threes?"

"It's slang for 'good luck'."

Five minutes later, Pop's walkie-talkie snapped back to life.

"Signal, this is Detail Leader with Renegade," the White House Secret Service agent radioed. "Copy."

"Ten-four," Signal replied.

"Renegade's finished his call with General Jones and is back in a sand trap on the second hole," Detail Leader said. "Copy."

"Come again?" Signal said. "Copy."

"I said Renegade's back on the golf course," Detail Leader said. "Copy."

"Renegade's *back* on the course after the *terrorist* attack?" Signal said. "Copy."

"That a big ten-four," Detail Leader said.

"No, it isn't," Signal said. "That's a big negatory."

The transmission ended.

Pop looked at me and rolled his eyes. "I suppose you want to know what a 'negatory' is."

"I can guess," I said.

Just then, one of Sasha and Malia's friends, a girl named Nancy, started screaming. Vangie and Pop flew out of their beach chairs and sprinted down to the water. I was right behind them.

When I got there, I saw that Bo, in his excitement, had gotten carried away and inadvertently bitten Nancy's finger. It was bleeding profusely, and the frightened little girl was sobbing inconsolably.

Vangie tried to calm her down; she held her thumb and index finger over Nancy's cut to stem the bleeding.

"There-there, Nance, it's OK," Vangie said. "You'll be fine. We've got a first-aid kit. Let's go find a Band-Aid."

"Where's the White House physician?" I asked Pop as we trudged through the sand back to the rented house.

"With Renegade," he said.

At the house, Vangie opened a white metal box with a Red Cross on the side and rummaged around until she found a Band-Aid. She tore it open and was about to apply it to Nancy's cut finger.

"No!" Nancy shouted, pulling her hand away. "I want a Mickey Mouse Band-Aid! I want *Mickey!*"

"What'll we do?" Vangie asked Pop.

"Let me try something," Pop said.

He keyed his walkie-talkie. "Detail Leader, this is Beach," he said. "We have a situation. The First Dog has bitten one of the First Daughters' friends. I want to repeat—this is *not* one of the First Daughters but one of their friends. She insists on a Mickey

Mouse Band-Aid. Can you contact the White House physician? Copy."

"Ten-four," Detail Leader said. "Stand by. Copy"

A minute later, Detail Leader came back on.

"Beach, this is Detail Leader. Renegade and his entire party have stopped playing golf and are convoying to you right now. Copy."

"Come again?" Pop said. "Renegade is on his way back to the house? Copy."

"That's a big ten-four," Detail Leader said.

"Why?" Pop said. "Copy."

"To locate a Band-Aid for his daughter's friend," Detail Leader said.

I looked at Pop, who was shaking his head in bewilderment.

"The President won't stop playing golf after a terrorist attack," he said, "but he drops everything and rushes back here to find a Band-Aid?"

"Not just any Band-Aid, Pop," Vangie said. "A *Mickey Mouse* Band-Aid."

Ten minutes later, sirens alerted us to the arrival of the presidential motorcade. Barack Obama, dressed in a blue golf hat, white shirt, khaki golf shorts, and golf shoes, clattered into the house with the White House physician on his heels. The doctor examined the girl's cut finger.

"Honey," he told Nancy, "this isn't a very deep wound. But we've got to put a Band-Aid on it."

"I only want a Mickey Mouse Band-Aid," she said.

The doctor looked up at Barack Obama.

"Mr. President," he said, "I'm sorry, but I don't carry Mickey Mouse Band-Aids."

"Then we'll just have to go *find* one, won't we?" the President said. "C'mon, girls. Vangie, you come, too."

He looked at me, and a flash of recognition crossed his face. "Bring John along, too. You can't have too much tactical planning."

"His name's Higgy," Vangie said.

We all piled into the presidential limousine. I sat up front with the Secret Service driver. The girls and Vangie sat on the jump seats in the back with the President.

"Mr. President," the driver asked, "where to?"

"The nearest Rite Aid drug store," the President said.

The motorcade zoomed out the driveway, followed by several cars carrying members of the print and TV media. We headed to a nearby strip mall and skidded to a stop in front of a Rite Aid store. As a team of Secret Service agents fanned out to keep curiosity seekers back at a safe distance, the president, Vangie, the four girls, four more agents, and I—a total of eleven people—strode into the store. TV cameramen rushed in after us, knocking several customers aside.

"Do you carry Mickey Mouse Band-Aids?" the president asked the pharmacist.

"N-n-no, M-Mr. Obama," the pharmacist stuttered, practically struck dumb by the presence of the president of the United States. "But w-w-we *do* have Hannah Montana Band-Aids."

"Nancy," the President said, "how does Hannah Montana grab you?"

"I only want Mickey!" Nancy cried.

"She only wants Mickey," the president repeated. "Okay then," he barked in full commander-in-chief mode, "everybody back to the car. Let's try a Duane Reed."

And so it went for the next hour and a half—a presidential chase at breakneck speed, with sirens blasting away and the media in hot pursuit. Local motorcycle cops joined the convoy, adding their sirens to the cacophony. We visited Duane Reeds, Walmarts, Kmarts Targets, and a Drug Store Inc.—until we found a box of Mickey Mouse Band-Aids in an Overstock Drug Store.

While the TV cameras recorded the event, the White House physician bandaged Nancy's finger. A few minutes later, the presidential motorcade dropped us back at the rented house.

"Okay," the President announced, "off to the golf course. We'll pick up where we were—on the sixth green. I'm laying three there."

And his motorcade roared off.

CHAPTER FIFTY-FOUR

On orders from Whitney Nutwing, I flew overnight on a MITT jet from Honolulu to the University of Michigan Hospital in Ann Arbor to be present when Attorney General Eric Holder Jr. personally interrogated Umar Farouk Abdulmutallab, otherwise known as "The Underwear Bomber."

I walked into a secure wing of the hospital and was escorted to a heavily guarded room. Inside was a young man lying in a hospital bed with tubes and wires attached to various parts of his body. Sitting next to him was the attorney general in a sweater and without a necktie. Holder had an earpiece in his right ear and a remotely controlled video camera hung from the ceiling.

"Mr. Abdulmutallab," Holder said to the man in the bed, "this interview is being tape recorded. After consulting with the FBI, the CIA, the Director of National Intelligence, and the Secretary of Homeland Security, I decided you should be read your Miranda rights. Here in America, you don't have to say anything that might incriminate you."

"But …I… *want*…to…talk," Abdulmutallab said in halting English. "I…have…much…to…say…"

Holder put his hand up to his ear and adjusted his earpiece. He appeared to be listening to an invisible observer.

"If this fellow *wants* to talk," I told Holder, "don't you want to hear what he has to say?"

"Depends," Holder said.

"There…are…others…in Yemen…others who…" Abdulmutallab began.

"Hold your horses!" Holder shouted.

Again, he paused to listen to someone talk to him through the earpiece.

"Don't you want the information that this guy can provide?" I asked.

"Only if it is obtained through proper legal procedure," Holder said.

"This *is* proper legal procedure," I said. "He *wants* to talk."

Holder looked up at the camera and nodded his head.

"I'm not so sure," he said. "A judge might say he was under the influence of pain medications and thus the"—and he made quotation marks with the fingers of each hand—"*admissibility* of his answers would be called into question."

"Eric, maybe you should be representing this guy as his *defense attorney*," I said. "You're doing a better job of stopping him from talking than Johnnie Cochran did for O.J. Simpson!"

Holder listened to the voice in his earpiece and then said, "It's all about procedure. The letter of the law."

"What if there are others in Yemen with Umar here?" I asked. "What if they're about to attack the United States? Any information he can give us might prevent thousands of casualties, now or in the future."

"There...*are*...others!" Abdulmutallab said. "Please ... tell... him... to... let... me... talk. I...have...information..."

"*Stop!*" Holder shouted. "Stop at once! You haven't waived your right to speak."

"Yes...yes...there...*is*...a...*wave*...of...other...suicide... bombers... coming...from...Yemen..." Abdulmutallab said.

"We don't want to hear this!" Holder said. 'This session is over. I hope he hasn't said too much."

"Thanks to you, he hasn't said *anything*!" I protested.

"Higginbothem," Holder said, "someone wants to talk to you."

Holder yanked the earpiece out of his ear and handed it to me.

I stuck it into my right ear and heard a familiar voice.

"John, I thought you were *my* Baptist." It was President Barack Obama. "Some John the Baptist you've turned out to be."

All my *constructive thinking* suddenly left me.

"Mr. President," I said, "I thought I *was* representing you. This Underwear Bomber has information about other imminent attacks that we may be able to prevent if we allow him to talk."

Suddenly, I heard the voice of Chief of Staff Rahm Emanuel. He screamed into my earpiece.

"How *dare* you question the judgment of President Obama? Who the fuck do you think you are? Barack Obama knows *more* than ten other men put together. You're done! Through! *Out!* I told that Fat Fuck Nutwing that he'll be out on his gigantic fucking ass, too, if he doesn't cut you loose! So good fucking goodbye, you motherfucking asshole. You're fucking fired!"

And with that rather unceremonial dismissal, my career at the CIA came to a rather sudden and unexpected end.

CHAPTER FIFTY-FIVE

One week later, Taitsie and I stood on the snowy dock of the Yacht Club overlooking Provincetown Harbor. The Pilgrims had briefly dropped anchor here in 1620. This was where the first English settlers had signed the Mayflower Compact before setting sail again for Plymouth Rock. And this, I thought, was a fitting place for Taitsie and me to reaffirm the marriage compact that *we* had signed almost twenty-five years before.

The Deuce and Vier stood next to me, while Taitsie's parents, Elizabeth and "Ducky" Millard, stood next to her. Vangie, Russ, Sydney Michael Green, and Elvira—who had flown in overnight from Chicago—were also in attendance.

Just as we were assembling for the ceremony, the Desert Girls showed up. They walked onto the dock, arm-in-arm, in matching full-length fur coats. Before taking their places, they gave Taitsie a buss on the cheek and shook my hand. I greeted them with a warm smile. Maybe my chance with them wasn't over, after all.

Taitsie had rounded up a female minister from a local women's commune, and asked her to preside over our recommitment ceremony.

"Everyone, please gather around and take the hand of the person next to you," the minister said as she took my left hand and Taitsie's right hand in hers. "We are here to re-affirm the solemn vows taken here in Provincetown by Theodore and Elizabeth back in 1986.

"Do you both vow to remain loyal and true to each other until the day you die?" she continued.

"Yes," Taitsie said.

"Yes," I said. "And I can vow one more thing. There will be no more secrets between us."

This time around I wasn't going to do *anything* to endanger our marriage. No more drinking and no more CIA. God had given me this second chance, and I wasn't going to blow it.

The minister then said, "Congratulations on your mutual wisdom to realize that you belong with each other."

She reached into her pocket and pulled out an envelope and handed it to Taitsie.

"This is your Re-Affirmation Certificate," the minister said. "Keep it where you both can see it often, and it will serve as a reminder of your devotion to each other."

As the guests applauded, a large yacht came around the point and headed toward our dock. The manager of the yacht club emerged from his office and approached our group.

"This just arrived for you," he said.

He handed me a large manila envelope with my name printed on the front in Cyrillic script.

I opened it and found a short, hand-written note.

> Dear Comrade Higgy,
>
> Congratulations on the recommitment of your wedding vows – and on your departure from our profession. As a sign of my affection for you, I enclose the deed to my special gift to you and Mrs. Higgy.
>
> With affection,
> Yurik Maligin

Attached was a three-page legal document giving me ownership of Maligin's yacht, *The Escape.*

Just then, *The Escape's* horn sounded with a series of three long, festive, celebratory blasts—*VROOM... VROOM... VROOM*—followed by a round of fireworks launched from the deck.

The Escape—with its two helicopters, two swimming pools, a mini-submarine, an anti-missile system, an anti-paparazzi shield, and a crew of sixty—came to a stop right behind us.

The Escape was the perfect name for our honeymoon ship. Taitsie and I climbed the walkway, and were greeted by the same tall, beautiful Russian blonde ship's officer, Yelena, who had welcomed me aboard almost five years ago in Mombasa Harbor.

"Congratulations to you both, Mr. and Mrs. Higginbothem," she said. "Welcome aboard. I have the delivery you ordered."

"Where is *she*?" I asked.

"*Hier bin ich*—Here I am," said the Countess Gladys of Thurn und Taxis as she emerged from the pilothouse. "And vere ist Meester Sydney?"

Standing by the rail, I called down to Sydney Michael Green. I no longer cared if Syd had tried to undercut me. He was no longer my problem. I had forgiven him for—well, for everything.

"Syd," I said, "I'm sending you the countess. I know how you two feel about each other, and I hope you will be as happy as Taitsie and I."

The countess ran down the gangplank and into the waiting arms of Sydney Michael Green. I knew she would keep him happy and living the high life in Europe.

On the yacht, we waved to our family and friends on the dock below. Our son stood next to The Deuce, who was going to keep Vier on his west Texas farm. The Deuce intended to homeschool Vier in the craft of espionage.

As it turned out, Vier wanted to be the next Theodore J. Higginbothem and join the CIA. Given my current persona non grata status, it remained to be seen whether the CIA would have him. But it was my guess that by the time Vier was old enough to join the CIA, the Obama/Rahm Emanuel grudge against the Higginbothems would be a thing of the past.

The Escape's engines thrummed beneath us, and we were off. As we rounded the point and headed out to sea, Taitsie turned to me.

"Well, Bottom," she said, "I think it's time for some *Sie müssen aufhören!*"

"What's that?" I asked with a wink.

She gave my hand a loving squeeze. "Let's go below and I'll show you."

CHAPTER FIFTY-SIX

For the next two months, Taitsie and I enjoyed a second honeymoon aboard our new yacht. As *The Escape* crisscrossed the warm waters of the South Atlantic Ocean, we settled into a pleasant, unvarying routine. Soon, it became hard to tell one day from another.

We converted the main lounge into Taitsie's sculpture studio. There, dressed in a smock over her bikini, she worked with tools and clay that we purchased on a brief provisioning stopover in Huelva, Spain. As for me, I spent most of the daylight hours toiling over the manuscript of this book, banging out the chapters on my old Smith Corona Sterling 12 manual typewriter. Because of the CIA's Publications Review Board's prohibition against revealing classified material, I found two complete losers—Edward Klein and John LeBoutillier—and convinced them to put their names on this book.

Without fail, my GlobalStar GSP 1600 satellite phone would begin beeping during the evening cocktail hour. It was always The Deuce, calling us on an encrypted line. He would say a few words and then put Vier on the phone. Hearing our son's voice, we were reassured he was safe and sound.

After dinner, Taitsie and I read out loud to each other (usually something from Dickens or Trollope) until our eyes grew heavy. Then, if we felt like it, which we usually did, we would make love. Afterward, spent and happy, we had a little ritual. I would turn out the lights, take Taitsie in my arms, kiss her softly on the lips, and repeat the same words every night.

"Darling girl," I said, "I've never been happier in my life. I love you."

"Bottom," came Taitsie's invariable reply, "me, too*!*"

CHAPTER FIFTY-SEVEN

On a late March Sunday morning, 440 nautical miles north-northeast of Tierra del Fuego, Taitsie and I were sunbathing on the foredeck when Yelena, the blonde ship's officer, came running toward us in a state of high anxiety.

"Mr. Higgy! Mr. Higgy! We have a visitor!"

She pointed off to the starboard side of *The Escape*. No more than a hundred yards away, emerging from the deep like some giant orca whale, was the USS *Annapolis*, a Los Angeles-class long-range nuclear attack submarine.

Four sailors appeared on deck and carefully lowered a corpulent figure into a small inflatable Zodiac rubber boat. They motored over to *The Escape*, and several of our crewmembers helped Whitney Nutwing climb aboard.

He looked terrible. His face had a greenish pallor and there were dark circles under his eyes. He was even heavier than the last time I had seen him, and he had trouble catching his breath.

"Higgy…Taitsie…" he said, gasping for air. "How are you?"

"Fine—until *now*," I said. "In view of your lack of support for me when I was fired by Rahm Emanuel, you'll pardon me if I don't pretend that I'm overjoyed to see you."

"I understand," Nutwing said. "So let me get straight to the point. Since you left the CIA, Higgy, things have gone to hell in a handbasket. President Obama has squandered his popularity and has negative poll numbers. He's become desperate. At his insistence, the White House has commissioned a top-secret study by the Army Corps of Engineers, codenamed OPERATION FACELIFT."

"For what?" I asked.

"For Obama," Nutwing said. "They want to carve President Obama's face on Mount Rushmore, right next to Abe Lincoln's."

"So what's the big problem?"

"Obama's ears don't fit on the side of the mountain."

"What's all that have to do with Taitsie and me?" I asked.

"Higgy," Nutwing said, "as Obama loses his mojo, he's been getting some really strange ideas! Maligin has him over a barrel. The United States is naked unto its enemies, if you'll excuse the biblical reference. For example, Obama's back schmoozing those crazy mullahs in Iran while they're furiously racing to build nukes. He's caved into Russia on a missile-reduction treaty. He's going wobbly on China, afraid to confront them because they hold all our debt. And he even wants to open relations with the Castro brothers!"

Nutwing was starting to hyperventilate.

"Again, let me repeat: who gives a damn?" I told him. "None of this has *anything* to do with me and Taitsie."

"Higgy, please! We want you and the entire Tchaikovsky Circle to come back. We *need* you. We want you to do what only *you* can do: save America from Barack Obama!"

Just then my GlobalStar GSP 1600 satellite phone beeped. I looked at the LED screen and didn't recognize the number.

"Yes?" I answered.

"Please hold for the director," said a female voice on the other end.

A click—and Leon Panetta, the director of the Central Intelligence Agency, came on the line.

"Mr. Higginbothem, do not – I repeat do *not* – acknowledge me by my name or my position. If you understand this just say, 'Hello, Dad.'"

"Hello, Dad," I said.

Taitsie refilled Nutwing's iced-tea glass and began some meaningless chitchat with him about equestrian riding. That was a laugh. If Nutwing ever got up on a horse, he'd break the nag's back. I walked up to the bow of *The Escape* so that I'd be out of earshot.

"Mr. Higginbothem," Panetta said, "Higgy, if I may…this is a delicate matter. The CIA *needs* you and your Tchaikovsky Circle back as soon as possible. However, after dispatching Whitney Nutwing to persuade you of the urgency of the matter, it dawned on me that *he*, not *you*, may be the *real* impediment."

"What do you mean?" I asked.

"Here is what I'm offering you," Panetta said. "I'll retire Nutwing at once and relocate him to his beloved Rome, where he can speak Italian to his heart's content. You'll never see him again. And, Higgy, I am offering *you* Nutwing's job. You will oversee *all* our clandestine *domestic* political activities, reporting only to me. Your Tchaikovsky Circle will remain intact and report to you."

After Whitney Nutwing was back on the USS *Annapolis*, Taitsie and I stood, hand in hand, exchanging light smooches, and watched the gigantic nuclear submarine disappear under the sea.

"Taitsie," I said, still holding her hand, "that satellite phone call was from Leon Panetta, urging me to return to the CIA and offering me Nutwing's job."

"Sounds tempting," she said. "*Are* you tempted?"

"Taitsie, there are three things I believe in," I said. "First, you and Vier. My love for you and our son means everything to me. During those years of separation, I realized I couldn't live without you."

She squeezed my hand a bit harder.

"Second, I believe in God," I said. "I wouldn't be alive and here with you today without that faith. I would be a useless, selfish, aimless alcoholic. Believing in a Higher Power has humbled me. And, believe me, I needed humbling."

I paused for a moment and then continued.

"And third, I believe with all my heart in the United States of America. Whatever may be wrong with our country, whatever may be wrong with its corrupt and venal politicians, we are privileged to live in America. When I joined the CIA, I thought it was the best way to serve my country. But after recent events, I wonder if I made a huge mistake."

Taitsie and I watched three seagulls glide gently over *The Escape*. The Atlantic was calm. The sun was hot. And there was a light breeze.

"Bottom," Taitsie said at last, "you still haven't answered my question. *Are* you tempted to go back?"

I looked at this beautiful woman, who still filled me with excitement and passion after more than twenty-five years of marriage.

"As I told you when we recommitted ourselves," I said, "there will be no more secrets between us. So whatever *I* may want to do will only happen if we want to do it *together*."

Taitsie scoffed at that sentiment. "Bottom, I never had a problem with your working for the CIA," she said. "It was the not knowing *why* you were away, the not knowing *why* you would not tell me *what* you were doing or where you were going. The not knowing *who* you were with and *when*."

"I understand."

"So," she said, "what will it be? Sail the seven seas? Or go back now and serve your country?"

For a moment I could not reply. I'd become used to wandering aimlessly over the seven seas, not shaving, not primping, allowing the total lazy bum inside me to ride this horse. At the thought of going back, I wanted nothing more than to heave the weighty cares of the world into the rocking waves.

"Who knows?" I said. "Now's not the time to decide such matters. Now's the time for *Sie müssen aufhören!*"

THE END